CRAP KITCHEN

Boiled gannet,
calf-brain custard and
other 'acquired tastes'

Geoff Tibballs

D1464356

ROBINSON

ROBINSON

First published in Great Britain in 2015
by Robinson

Copyright © Geoff Tibballs, 2015

1 3 5 7 9 10 8 6 4 2

The moral right of the author has been
asserted.

A CIP catalogue record for this book
available from the British Library.

ISBN: 978-1-47213-681-7 (paperback)

Design & typesetting by Andrew Barron

Illustrations copyright © The Brothers
McLeod 2015

Printed and bound in Great Britain by
Clays Ltd, St Ives plc

Papers used by Robinson are from well-
managed forests and other responsible
sources.

MIX
Paper from
responsible sources
FSC® C104740

Robinson
is an imprint of
Little, Brown Book Group
Carmelite House
50 Victoria Embankment
London EC4Y 0DZ

Contents

Introduction

Ever since Neanderthal Man first discovered that the flesh of animals, birds and sea creatures had the potential for making a more substantial meal than leaves and berries and also went much better with a nice Merlot, the culinary world has produced some staggering creations which could best be described as 'acquired tastes'.

The Roman Empire was built on such delicacies as boiled flamingo, grilled cow's womb and calf brain custard while a favourite roast dish in Tudor England was cockenthrice where the head and upper body of a pig was carefully stitched on to the lower body and legs of a turkey. Meanwhile in Switzerland it used to be traditional to eat cats at Christmas, giving rise to the Swiss saying 'A pet is not just for Christmas – if you're lucky there'll be some left over for Boxing Day'.

When the Prussian Army encircled Paris in 1870, cutting off food supplies, as many as 70,000 horses in the city were slaughtered for their meat. Champion racehorses did not survive the chop either and when the supply of horse was exhausted, chefs got creative with vermin and pets.

One Latin Quarter menu offered:

Consommé de cheval au millet
(horse soup with millet)

Brochettes de foie de chien à la maître d'hôtel
(dog liver)

Emincés de râbles de chat sauce mayonnaise
(sliced saddle of cat with mayo)

Epaule de filet de chien sauce tomate
(shoulder of dog in a tomato sauce)

Civet de chat aux champignons
(cat stew with mushrooms)

Côtelettes de chien aux petits pois
(dog chops with peas)

Salmis de rat à la Robert
(rat stew)

Gigots de chien flanqués de ratons avec sauce poivrade
(dog leg with a pepper sauce and rat garnish)

Plum pudding au rhum et à la Moelle de Cheval
(plum pudding with horse marrow sauce)

As the siege entered a third month at the end of the year, hungry Parisians turned their attention to the city zoo where the animals were no longer able to be fed. Antelope, camels, yaks and zebras were the first to be killed and even the zoo's two elephants, Castor and Pollux, ended up at the dinner table. A butcher named Deboos paid 27,000 francs for the pair and went on to sell the various body parts for up to 14 francs a pound with the trunks fetching as much as 45 francs a pound. Unlikely as it may seem, someone had obviously tasted elephant before and considered the trunk to be a delicacy. However, the general impression was distinctly underwhelming. One diner complained that his slice of elephant was 'tough, coarse and oily' and not a patch on beef or mutton. It was with some irony therefore that elephant meat was declared to be totally forgettable.

A few zoo animals were spared. Monkeys were considered to be so close to humans that eating them would be akin to cannibalism; lions and tigers were too dangerous to approach and kill, and the hippopotamus escaped because the price of 80,000 francs demanded for it was too expensive for any butcher. Thus a Christmas menu in an upmarket Parisian restaurant for the ninety-ninth day of the siege offered such mouth-watering festive dishes as stuffed donkey's head, elephant consommé, roast camel, kangaroo stew, antelope terrine, bear ribs, and wolf haunch in deer sauce. Fortunately the establishment still had some expensive wines in the cellar to mask the taste.

Today there are dozens of traditional local dishes adding weight to the old adage that one man's meat is another man's poison. Those with an adventurous mindset and a robust life insurance policy can eat yak penis and tuna eyeball (China), the still-beating heart of a freshly killed snake (Vietnam), sheep's head (Norway), raw puffin heart (Iceland), fried tarantula (Cambodia), duck embryo (Philippines), boiled gannet (Scotland's Western Isles), bull's testicles (United States) or mouse kebabs (Malawi), perhaps followed by some live maggot-infested cheese from Sardinia and washed down by a bottle of *Ttongsul*, a Korean wine made from human faeces.

So why not try some of the unusual and often challenging recipes listed here? If only to ensure that certain dinner party guests will never visit again.

Disclaimer: *The author absolves himself of all responsibility should anyone preparing any of the dishes featured in this book end up dissatisfied, divorced or in A&E. Recipes have been reproduced faithfully according to their sources, so both metric and imperial measurements are used.*

Duck embryo

PHILIPPINES

Unsuspecting diners about to tackle *balut* for the first time might be forgiven for thinking they are breaking into a Kinder Surprise. But instead of a toy, this egg houses a more grotesque surprise – a partially developed duck embryo, which you are then expected to eat straight from the shell. In the Philippines, *balut* has graduated from street food to haute cuisine, although it is frequently also used as a hangover cure. Perhaps the theory is that if anything is likely to dissuade you from getting drunk in future, it is the prospect of having to eat *balut* afterwards.

The fertilized duck eggs are stored in baskets in the sun so that they stay warm. After nine days, they are held up to a light to check that there is an embryo inside. If there is, then approximately eight days later they are ready to be eaten. Filipinos believe *balut* to be at its best at seventeen days old because it is 'wrapped in white'. At that stage the chick inside the egg is not quite old enough to have grown a beak, feathers or claws, and its bones are underdeveloped. However in Vietnam, where the dish is equally popular, they prefer to wait for another few days until the chick is actually recognizable as a baby duck and has bones that will be firm but tender when cooked. When eating *balut* in Vietnam, try not to think about the beak sticking in your throat.

Balut is the dish that keeps on giving. It comes in four parts – the yolk, the amniotic fluid, the albumen and, of course, the embryo itself. There are a number of different ways to consume boiled *balut*, few of which do not require keeping your eyes closed. *Balut* connoisseurs recommend first making a small hole in the rounder end of the shell, then breaking through the membranes and drinking the warm broth-like fluid that surrounds the embryo, as this is said to be the tastiest part, before tackling the chick itself. Others choose to begin by scooping out the yolk, veins and all. Depending on the age of the egg, the white albumen at the bottom of the shell may be tough and rubbery, although if you have managed to get this far you will probably not be overly concerned.

For those with strong stomachs, a Filipino restaurant in New York stages an annual balut eating contest at which the winner has been known to down 27 in five minutes. The runner-up was literally spitting feathers.

INGREDIENTS

● 1 fertilized duck egg
● A sprinkling of salt
● Chopped garlic
● ½ cup of vinegar

METHOD

Hard-boil the duck egg for 20–30 minutes and crack open part of the shell with a spoon. Remove the section of shell and devour the contents. Alternatively you may prefer to extricate the baby bird and dip it in salt or a warm garlic and vinegar sauce. Either way, you're still eating a duck fetus.

Recipe: *www.travelchannel.com*

Still-beating snake heart

VIETNAM

Whereas the world's leading restaurants are rated by the number of Michelin stars they have, certain establishments in the Le Mat district of Hanoi are best judged on the number of snake bites on the waiters' arms and legs. For this is 'Snake Village' where cobra is the dish of every day and the fewer the bite scars on the waiter's body, the better the chances are that your meal will have died a relatively swift death. Conversely, if the waiter has a couple of fingers missing, it might be advisable to search elsewhere.

Ever since the release of the Leonardo DiCaprio movie *The Beach* in 2000 popularized the drinking of snake blood among young people in search of the ultimate travel experience, it has apparently become a rite of passage for western backpackers visiting northern Vietnam – and with the added twist of also eating the dead snake's still-beating heart. Indeed many of Hanoi's hostels offer special excursions where tourists can watch in a mixture of disbelief and apprehension as their waiter kills and guts a snake – usually an angry, hissing cobra – at their table. Sometimes the snake's venom is removed beforehand, thus denying the creature a realistic chance of retribution, but other waiters prefer to drain it into a bottle after the reptile has been beheaded. This is a wise precaution as chefs have been known to be killed by a bite from the severed head of a snake as long as twenty minutes after it has been cut off. The venom can then be drunk as it is only poisonous when taken intravenously. At least that's what they tell you.

Customers are invited to select their own snake for consumption but many are happy to leave the choice to the waiter. In Le Mat, recommending a good snake comes as naturally to a waiter as recommending a good wine. One blogger described the whole experience thus: 'When you've selected the tastiest-looking snake, the host will pull it out of the cage, throw it on the floor and start poking it with a stick. If it starts hissing like a punctured tyre and tries to kill everyone in the room, you're good to go.'

The dish acquires its unique appeal from the fact that a snake's heart often continues to beat for several minutes after death and the waiters pander to the visitors' sense of bravado by telling them that consuming snake heart is 'good for big willy'. Then again, virtually every product in south-east Asia is claimed to enhance virility. However, animal welfare authorities in Vietnam unsurprisingly consider the practice to be barbaric and point out that it is not even a genuine Vietnamese tradition but rather one that has been created pretty much solely for the tourist industry.

The one consolation is that no part of the snake goes to waste. After swallowing the beating heart, the remaining courses are marginally more palatable – snake soup, roast snake ribs, snake spring rolls, snake meatballs, fillet of snake, snake tail with crispy lemongrass and crispy fried snake skin. Inevitably it is said to taste like chicken.

Eat your heart out.

INGREDIENTS
● 1 live snake

METHOD
Insert a knife just underneath the snake's head, cut it off and drain the venom if necessary. Slit the snake open lengthways, scoop out the heart and eat it while it is still beating. It is probably best to swallow the heart in one firm gulp instead of chewing on it, as the latter course of action would only serve to remind you of what you are actually doing. They say you can feel the heart beating as it slides down your throat. This is not a comforting thought. Should you require a drink to accompany the snake heart, it is recommended that you squeeze the snake's blood and gall bladder into two glasses of rice wine and down those. The glass with the blood remains red while that with the bile from the gall bladder turns an alarming shade of green. For a full-on experience, you can put the snake heart in the same glass as the blood or the bile. Fortunately the rice wine is so strong that it tends to overpower the taste of snake innards. Even so, before attempting this local delicacy it is probably best to be considerably more inebriated than the average newt.

Calf brain custard

ANCIENT ROME

This recipe for savoury custard originally appeared in the Apicius Roman cookbook, believed to have been compiled between the first and fourth centuries AD. At least three famous foodies of the time bore the name Apicius, leading to confusion as to which (if any) was responsible for the collection. A number of sources cite Marcus Gavius Apicius, a renowned gourmet during the reign of Tiberius (AD 14–37). Pliny stated that Apicius was a particular champion of flamingo's tongue. According to legend, Apicius spent his entire fortune on food before taking his own life because he was down to his last 10 million *sestertii* and feared that he would eventually run out of money and face starvation. Stylish to the last, he took poison at a banquet specifically arranged for his exit.

Since the Apicius cookbook contains recipes for thrush, dormouse and sow's womb, calf brain custard was in no way considered extreme. Adopting the maxim that you are what you eat, many Romans believed that eating brains would enhance their intelligence. To this end, the emperor Heliogabalus had 600 ostrich brains prepared for one banquet, presumably having first managed to extricate them from the sand. The Romans loved the bitter taste of rose petals and also considered them to be an aphrodisiac. So a combination of sex and brains proved irresistible to Roman chefs, especially those who had been hired to do the catering for an orgy. Ninety per cent of Roman recipes featured *garum*, a pungent relish made from the guts of fish that had been left to ferment in the sun for three months. *Garum* was also used to treat everything from dog bites to chronic diarrhoea and even to remove unwanted body hair and freckles. It was nothing if not versatile. Since *garum* is sadly no longer available you will need to substitute it here with a strong fish sauce.

Heston Blumenthal is not one to shy away from a culinary challenge, but when he prepared calf brain custard for his 2009 TV show *Heston's Roman Feast*, the kindest thing he could say about the concoction was that it tasted nowhere near as bad as it smelled.

INGREDIENTS

- Two handfuls of rose petals
- ¾ pint of fish sauce
- 4 calf brains
- 8 scruples (10g) of pepper
- 8 eggs
- ¾ pint of wine
- 1 glass of raisin wine
- A little oil

METHOD

Remove the white areas at the base of the rose petals, put the remainder of the petals in a mortar, pour on the fish sauce and pound to crush the petals. Strain the liquid through a colander or sieve. Skin and remove the sinews from the calf brains and chop the brains into small cubes. Crush the pepper, pour the rose liquid over the brains and pound again until all the meat is ground to a pulp. Break and beat the eggs, add the wine and the raisin wine plus the oil. Grease a dish, pour in the mixture and cook for 30 minutes at 350°F (180°C). Season with pepper and serve. Hold your nose and your nerve.

Recipe: *Cooking and Dining in Imperial Rome* by Apicius

Tuna eyeball

JAPAN

If you have ever felt guilty about being a carnivore, tuna eyeball probably isn't for you. Unfathomably large and dark, it can be found staring eerily back at you in most Japanese stores for less than a pound and the prospect of picking it up with chopsticks and holding it your mouth can turn even the strongest stomach. Sold surrounded in fish fat and severed muscles, it has a rich, fatty flavour, although the wall of the eyeball possesses a distinctly rubbery texture. If you can get past the fact that you're eating an eyeball, it's actually not too bad.

Although it is often served in sushi bars, you should not eat it raw as it can collect bacteria all too easily. The recipe below is for sautéed eyeball but it can also be boiled, stewed or nailed to the front door to keep cold callers away.

INGREDIENTS
- 1 tablespoon of sesame oil
- 1 tablespoon of chopped fresh ginger
- 1 tuna eyeball
- 1 tablespoon of soy sauce
- 1 slice of lemon

METHOD

Heat the sesame oil in a pan until it is hot but not smoking. Add the fresh ginger and cook for roughly 2 minutes so that the ginger is translucent but not brown. Put in the tuna eyeball and cook for one minute with the eye facing up. Add the soy sauce and continue cooking the eye until most of the sauce has evaporated. Serve the tuna eye on a plate and garnish with lemon. Try not to get in a staring competition with it.

Recipe: *www.ehow.com*

Fried mopane worms

SOUTHERN AFRICA

Mopane worms are not worms at all, but caterpillars, the larvae of the emperor moth. As long as a finger and as thick as a cigar, they get their name because they like to feed on the leaves of the mopane tree, and have become a popular delicacy across large areas of southern Africa. Highly nutritious and containing five times as much iron as you would find in beef, they can be fried with tomatoes and garlic, boiled and added to a stew or simply eaten raw fresh from the tree. Basically, if you like your grub, mopane worms are for you.

The best time to harvest them is when they are at their maximum plumpness, late in the larval stage, shortly before they transform into moths. Bags of dried or smoked mopane worms can be found on sale at markets in Botswana, Namibia, Zimbabwe, Zambia and northern parts of South Africa. Although they are a seasonal delicacy corresponding to the moth's life cycle, the worms can be bought in cans of brine at local supermarkets.

They have an unremarkable taste that has been compared to cardboard with a definite hint of timber, but this is swamped by the tomatoes and garlic when fried. When eaten fresh and raw, you can taste them in all their nondescript glory. They are less chewy when fresh but before popping one into your mouth, remember to pinch it at its tail end in order to rupture the innards.

You then squeeze it like a tube of toothpaste to force out the slimy, green contents of its gut. Only then is it ready to be eaten.

As well as providing an easily obtainable and cheap source of protein, the worms are a valuable source of income. At harvest time, hundreds of families hand-pick them from the trees before leaving them to dry in the sun and selling them to vendors. Mopane worms are even exported to some European countries. The Boma restaurant in Victoria Falls specializes in serving local dishes, including fried mopane worms, to tourists. Any visitor who eats at least one worm receives a special certificate. Generally speaking, wherever you are in the world, if you have a delicate stomach or are unsure about the terms of your medical insurance, it is probably best to avoid sampling any food for which you are awarded a certificate.

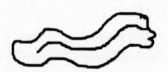

- 500g of dried mopane worms
- 2 diced onions
- ½ teaspoon of turmeric
- 3 fresh green chilies, finely chopped
- 3 cloves of garlic, finely chopped
- 1 tablespoon of fresh ginger, finely chopped
- 3 diced tomatoes or 1 can of tomatoes

METHOD

Soak the dried worms in water for between 3 and 4 hours.
Fry the onions in oil over a medium heat until translucent. Add
the turmeric, chillies, garlic and ginger. Fry for about 5 minutes.
Add the tomatoes and cook on low for about 20 minutes until the
spices are well blended. Add the drained worms and cook until
they have softened a little but are still a bit crunchy. Add salt and
pepper to taste. Serves four people.

Note: mopane is actually pronounced 'mopani'. It does not rhyme
with 'propane', which tastes considerably better.

Recipe: *yahoo.com*

Rotten shark

ICELAND

___

You might think there is no logical reason why anyone would choose to eat rotten meat but because Greenland shark meat is poisonous when fresh it makes perfect sense to Icelanders to eat it when it has fully decayed and all the toxic uric acid has been removed. The downside to this method of preparation is that by the time the fish is ready for consumption it smells strongly of ammonia. It is like eating a chunk of cleaning fluid.

Consequently, those tasting *hákarl* for the first time are advised to hold their nose beforehand to prevent gagging. After that, there is no need to worry. People rarely go back for a second piece.

It looks innocuous enough. The creamy-white cubes of fish are usually served on cocktail sticks accompanied by a shot of the local vodka-like spirit, *brennivin*, prompting food writer Mimi Aye to compare it to 'Seventies party food, if that party was held in Hell.' As for the stench, Aye said it resembled 'a tramp's sock soaked in urine'.

American chef Anthony Bourdain hailed *hákarl* as 'the single worst, most disgusting and terrible tasting thing' while his compatriot chef and food writer Andrew Zimmern described the smell as reminding him of 'some of the most horrific things I've ever breathed in my life'. He also warned ominously: 'That's hardcore.

That's serious food. You don't want to mess with that. That's not for beginners.' Alarmingly available in supermarkets, *hákarl* has also been given the dubious accolade of 'the world's most disgusting foodstuff that you can eat and still live'. So it seems putrefied shark meat is not to everyone's taste. Who would have thought it?

INGREDIENTS
- 1 dead shark
- 1 sharp knife or hatchet
- Cocktail sticks

METHOD

Gut and behead the shark and wash away the slime and blood. Cut the flesh into large pieces and place in a shallow hole in a sandy location – ideally a beach far from any homes to prevent residents being overpowered by the smell. Cover the shark with sand and gravel and place heavy stones on top of the sand in order to force the fluids out of the body. Allow the shark to rot in this manner for up to 3 months in winter or 7 weeks in summer. Next, hang the pieces up to dry for between 2 and 4 months. During this drying period, a brown crust will form. Finally, remove the crust, chop the shark meat into small cubes and serve on cocktail sticks as a challenging alternative to cheese and pineapple.

Recipe: *www.ifood.tv*

Bull's testicles

NORTH AMERICA

In North American ranching country, the castration of young cattle is commonplace at branding time in order to control breeding and improve temperament. The theory is that without all that testosterone coursing through its body the bull will develop into a much calmer animal and this will counteract any grudge it might be nursing due to the loss of its prize assets. The removed testicles are then thrown into a bucket of water before being turned into a popular snack among ranching families and at state festivals, where, to spare sensitivities, they appear under a variety of aliases. In the United States they are often called Rocky Mountain Oysters, in Canada they are known as Prairie Oysters, but you might also find them sold as Bull Fries, Dusted Nuts, Swinging Beef, Moo Marbles, Montana Tendergroins, Juicy Jewels or Cowboy Caviar. Despite the fancy names, the awful truth is you are still eating something that has spent its entire life hanging in a scrotum.

These tasty testes have been in circulation for a long time. With a pair coming off each animal, a rancher could end up with hundreds of testicles at the annual cattle castration. He might feed a few to his dogs as a reward, but the rest, rather than being tossed away, were destined for the dinner table, usually guzzled down with whisky or beer. A desire not to waste anything was only part of their appeal. Any self-respecting cowboy wanted to be the head of the herd, so what better way to make yourself irresistible to the ladies in the saloon on a Saturday night than by eating testosterone-filled bull's testicles – a dish seemingly guaranteed to help you win your spurs.

Edible testicles of all kinds – bull, sheep, pig and turkey – are celebrated throughout North America. Byron, Illinois, has staged a Turkey Testicle Festival since 1979, while the annual three-day Testicle Festival in Fargo, North Dakota, was the scene of a riot in 2001, leading to seven arrests, no doubt the result of too much testosterone. These gatherings are often fairly lively affairs. The event at Clinton, Montana – or the Testy Festy as it is known – is off limits to anyone under the age of twenty-one and includes oil wrestling, wet T-shirt competitions and 'No Panty Wednesday', when punters are offered a free drink in exchange for their underwear. Yet the real X-rated item on any testicle festival menu remains the food.

When they are deep fried in the traditional method you could be mistaken for thinking you were being served chicken nuggets. However, they have a slightly chewy texture and the taste has been variously likened to calamari, scallops and rattlesnake, the last a comparison that only a true cowboy would be able to make.

In truth, the biggest obstacle to overcome when eating Rocky Mountain Oysters is a mental one. Just remember, if you see them advertised on a menu, don't expect a dish of seafood.

INGREDIENTS
- 4 compliant bulls
- 2 eggs
- 2 cups of flour
- ½ cup of cornmeal
- Salt
- Pepper
- 1 cup of milk
- Cooking oil

METHOD

Peel the testicles by removing the tough, skin-like muscle that surrounds each one. Slice them into small ovals around half an inch thick. Beat the eggs and mix them in a bowl with the flour, cornmeal, salt and pepper. Roll each testicle piece in the flour mixture and dip into milk. Deep fry in hot oil for about 3 minutes until golden brown. Drain on paper towels and serve with a spicy sauce dip.

Recipe: *whatscookingamerica.net*

Fried tarantula

CAMBODIA

Towns and cities across the world lure tourists with different attractions. Paris has the Eiffel Tower, New York has the Empire State Building, Rome has the Colosseum – and Skuon, Cambodia, has fried tarantulas.

Poisonous tarantulas have long been used in Cambodian medicine because they were considered good for the heart, throat and lungs and also for building a healthy head of hair. Since they themselves are sufficiently hirsute to warrant a course of Veet, this is an understandable conclusion. However they only became part of local cuisine from the late 1970s when the country was under the rule of the notorious Khmer Rouge. Food at the time was in short supply, so people had to eat anything they could find. Tarantula fitted the bill. When Pol Pot's tyrannical regime came to an end, most Cambodians were only too happy to consign tarantulas to the garbage bin of history but the Skuonese had acquired a liking for them and maintained them as a regional delicacy.

The spiders, which are about the size of the palm of a hand, are bred in holes in the ground in nearby villages before being fried – fangs and all – in oil and sold for around $0.08 apiece. Children regard *a-ping*, as they are known locally, as a tasty snack in much the same way that British children might beg for a packet of cheese and onion crisps.

One spider hunter explained the method of extrication: 'There are two ways to get the spider out of its burrow. Usually we just dig them out, but it is also possible to push a stick down the hole and wait until the spider attacks. Then you pull it out.' An accomplished hunter, some of whom are as young as five, can catch several hundred spiders a day.

As you might expect should you have ever given the matter any thought, fried tarantula is crunchy on the outside and soft on the inside. There is little flesh on the legs but what they lack in substance they make up for in numbers. Meanwhile the head and body harbour a delicate white meat which has been compared to soft shell crab. The only section best avoided is the sizeable abdomen, which hangs ominously beneath the crispy legs and consists of a brown paste containing, among other things, spider excrement. Although some macho munchers claim this is the best part of the entire arachnid, even if you're not afraid of spiders, there is no shame in skirting around this particular body part. Spider-Man himself might be able to shoot webs from his wrists, scale tall buildings and fight crime on an industrial scale but beneath his mask even he would probably turn his nose up at the thought of eating deep-fried tarantula poo.

INGREDIENTS

- ½ cup of cornstarch
- ½ cup of flour
- ½ cup of milk
- 1½ teaspoons of baking powder
- ¾ teaspoon of salt
- ⅓ cup of water
- 6 tarantulas
- 1 clove of garlic
- 2 cups of vegetable oil

METHOD

Mix the cornstarch, flour, milk, baking powder, salt and water in a bowl and whisk until smooth. Singe off any fur from the tarantula legs, remove the abdomens if you so desire and dip the spiders in the batter mix so that each one is entirely coated. Spread out the legs to ensure total coverage. Crush a clove of garlic, heat the oil to 350°F (180°C) and fry the garlic in the oil until fragrant. Add the batter-covered spiders and fry in the garlic oil until the legs are almost completely stiff. Remove them from the oil and drain on paper towels. It is best to pull off the legs first and eat them two or three at a time rather than attempt to cram the whole tarantula into your mouth in one go.

Recipe: *www.epicurious.com*

Larks' tongues

ANCIENT ROME

___

Any recipe where the instructions begin with 'catch 1,000 larks' is likely to be a challenge to the amateur chef. However in ancient Rome the people who prepared such dishes employed slaves whose job for the day (or several days) would be to venture out into the fields and trap copious numbers of larks. Quite why the tongue of the lark was so prized in Roman cuisine is a mystery, but perhaps its beautiful song led the Romans to believe that its tongue must be particularly sweet. The argument was certainly good news for the crow.

According to contemporary sources, 1,000 larks was enough to serve only four people. Obviously a lark's tongue is tiny, but would you want to eat 250 of anything in one sitting? The Romans clearly didn't believe in small portions.

Flying in the face of most historians, one or two internet scholars have claimed that there is no firm evidence that the Romans ate larks' tongues, but this can surely be dismissed as songbird propaganda.

INGREDIENTS
- 1,000 larks
- 1 bottle of red wine

METHOD

Catch 1,000 larks. It is essential that they are caught alive to ensure that the meat is fresh. Prise open the mouth of each bird by folding back the upper beak and, using a sharp knife, cut out the tongue. Discard the remainder of the lark. Marinate the tongue in red wine overnight. Strain off the wine and serve. If the thought of eating uncooked larks' tongues is too awful to contemplate, you can also sauté them in a pan of hot oil.

Recipe: *Cooking and Dining in Imperial Rome* by Apicius

Raw puffin heart

ICELAND

With its colourful beak and clumsy behaviour, the puffin is without doubt one of the world's cutest birds. In Iceland, it is also regarded as one of the tastiest.

Puffins have been a source of sustenance for Icelanders for centuries. They catch the low-flying birds in a big net – a sport known as 'sky fishing' – and then break their necks, skin them and remove the heart, which they like to eat raw while it is still fresh and warm. No cooking required. Just a heart of stone. When celebrity chef Gordon Ramsay ate raw puffin heart on his TV show *The F Word* in 2008, a number of viewers complained about what they saw as callous cruelty. Others said watching Ramsay tuck in made them feel physically sick.

Puffin is not only eaten as an appetizer in Iceland. The whole bird or just the breast can also be smoked in blueberry sauce, grilled, pan-fried and served with gravy or boiled in milk. It is said to taste like a fishier version of duck, which is unsurprising considering its diet, although Ramsay described the meat as 'smooth on the palate and gamey, a bit like liver'.

INGREDIENTS (FOR PUFFIN IN MILK)

- 4 puffins
- Salt
- 50g of fatty bacon
- 50g of butter
- 300ml of milk
- 300ml of water

METHOD

Skin the puffins and remove the innards. Wash the birds thoroughly in cold water and rub with salt, both inside and out. Cut slits into the birds' breasts and draw strips of bacon through to ensure that the flesh will not be too dry. Truss the birds tightly so that they will fit into a cooking pot. Melt the butter in a cooking pot, stuff in the birds and brown on all sides. Heat the milk and water and pour over the puffins. Bring to the boil and then cook on low heat for between 1 and 1 ½ hours. Turn the birds occasionally in the pot and test for softness. Remove the birds and strain the cooking liquid. Serve your puffins with vegetables – you'll find that carrots are nicely colour co-ordinated with the beak.

Recipe: *icecook.blogspot.co.uk*

Virgin boy eggs

CHINA

How do you like your eggs? Scrambled, fried, poached? If you live in Dongyang, China, the chances are that your preference will be 'boiled and soaked in the urine of prepubescent schoolboys.'

Every springtime, buckets of urine from boys under the age of ten are collected from school toilets across the city. To ensure the purity of the urine, only healthy boys are allowed to pee in the specially designated buckets – any boy with a cold or other illness has to make his own arrangements. Vendors cook the eggs twice in pots of urine at roadside stalls, the all-too-familiar stench wafting over to passers-by. The cooking process takes almost an entire day and the vendors regularly add extra urine to prevent the eggs from overheating. They then sell them as a delicacy for $0.25 – double the price of ordinary eggs. They sell like hot cakes but sadly they don't taste like hot cakes.

With their, um, salty, flavour, virgin boy eggs – or *tong zi dan* as they are known locally – have been produced in the region for centuries and are said to possess remarkable health benefits. Nobody knows exactly how the custom originated or who first decided that eleven-year-old boys were unsuitable donors. The eggs are supposed to prevent heat stroke, improve blood circulation and generally rejuvenate the body. 'By eating these eggs, you will not have any pain in your waists, legs and joints,' says one enthusiastic customer. 'Also, you will have more energy when you work.' However, not everyone is keen on having the taste of pee in their mouth and some experts not only express grave doubts about the health claims but also warn of the sanitary hazards of eating food that has been cooked in a liquid by-product secreted by human kidneys.

The eggs are not only bought at street stalls. Some residents personally collect the boys' urine from local schools and cook the snack in their homes. If you can imagine a home where every child in a family of eight has wet the bed simultaneously, you will get some idea of how a Dongyang kitchen smells.

Probably the best thing that can be said about virgin boy eggs is that if you saw the item on a Chinese menu, you might fear you were about to eat children's testicles. Even for extreme Chinese cuisine, that would probably be a step too far.

INGREDIENTS
- 1 bucket of urine taken from prepubescent schoolboys
- 6 eggs

METHOD
Place the eggs in a medium saucepan and pour in the urine. Bring the eggs to the boil and then remove them from the pan with a strainer. Carefully crack the shells of the hard-boiled eggs and return them to the pan of urine. Cover the pan with a lid and allow the eggs to simmer on a low heat for around 10 hours. Peel away the shell and eat.

Recipe: *gizmodo.com*

Century eggs

CHINA

Although they are called century eggs or even thousand-year eggs, the name is misleading because these chicken, quail or duck eggs have actually been preserved for just a few months. The second shock is that when you come to eat the dish, the thing that sits before you looks nothing like any known egg. Traditionally kept in a mixture of salt, lime and ash, the egg has been transformed into something out of a sci-fi film. Your first thought is: didn't Doctor Who battle something similar in the last series? The chemical process it has undergone in storage has turned the yolk a mouldy dark green colour and the white of the egg dark brown and gelatinous. It could be mistaken for an overripe, slightly rotten avocado – until you smell it, that is. For it emits an odour that is a delightful mixture of ammonia and sulphur, like a cross between a piss and a fart. Consequently it often takes longer to pluck up the courage to break into a century egg than it does to eat it.

Century eggs date back over 600 years to the Ming Dynasty, when someone found some old eggs preserved in a pool of slaked lime.

On tasting them, he thought they were so good that he decided to produce some more, this time adding salt. In modern Chinese cuisine, they can be eaten straight from the shell as a snack or as an appetizer served with pickled ginger.

Nowadays they are mass produced in two months, using baking soda, salt and quicklime. However, in 2013 they were the subject of a food scare after thirty companies in Nanchang county, which manufactures 300,000 tons of century eggs annually, were closed down for using industrial copper sulphate instead of baking soda to speed up the maturing process to a month. Since copper sulphate contains arsenic, century eggs suddenly ran the risk of being even more toxic than they appear. One factory boss said reassuringly: 'There won't be a problem if you don't eat too many of them.'

The scare seems to have done little to affect the popularity of century eggs among Chinese people but not all visitors are convinced of their merits. CNN reporter Danny Holwerda described them as 'awful', adding: 'It tastes like the devil cooked eggs for me. It tastes like something that used to be an egg, but made some really horrible choices.'

INGREDIENTS

- 3lb of tea
- 7lb of wood ash
- 3lb of quicklime
- 9lb of sea salt
- 6 chicken, quail or duck eggs
- Rice husks

METHOD

Infuse the tea in boiling water so that it is strong and black. Mix the tea with the wood ash, quicklime and sea salt so that it forms a smooth paste. Wearing thick gloves to prevent the lime corroding your skin, cover each egg with a thick layer of the clay-like mixture. Then roll the eggs in a pile of rice husks in order to stop them sticking together while they are being stored. Place the eggs in cloth-covered jars and leave for about 3 months. When the mud mixture has dried and hardened into a crust, the eggs are ready for consumption. Better still, just buy them from a supermarket.

Recipe: *wikipedia*

Fruit bat soup

MICRONESIA

Just as you would not expect to find a whole chicken lying in a bowl of chicken soup or a tomato bobbing around in a bowl of tomato soup, when ordering fruit bat soup in a restaurant on the small Micronesian island of Palau, you would probably anticipate being greeted by nothing more sinister than a few chunks of meat and a broth. But be warned; in all probability you will be greeted by an entire bat, complete with fur, membranes, feet, wings and head (including a little pink tongue protruding through sharp teeth), floating lifelessly in your soup, looking to all intents and purposes as if it had recently drowned in a savoury swimming pool. As an appetizer, it looks anything but.

Some restaurants even allow you to choose your bat from a line-up before they cook it alive in boiling water. No sooner have you formed a relationship with it than you are eating it. If the waiter senses the horror on your face when confronted with a whole dead bat in your soup, he may kindly remove the bat, leave you with the soup, skin the bat and bring it back for you to eat the meat as a separate dish. Then again, he may call you a wimp and suggest you go to a McDonald's next time.

The sub-species of fruit bat known as the olik lives only on Palau.

It inhabits dense forest regions and spends most of its time hanging upside down in trees. Although this vantage point gives the bat a fabulous view of the magnificent landscape, it must also be disconcerting for it to look down and see a group of islanders entering the forest carrying nets and a large cooking pot.

As bats spend so much of their lives upside down, urine and faecal matter tend to cling to their bodies, so it is important to wash them well before use. Even so, there can still be a faint urine smell emanating from the bat's body while it is cooking but this should eventually be overwhelmed by the onion. The recipe below is a westerner-friendly version of the dish, in which the bat is skinned before serving. So there should be no need to floss away any bat fur that has got stuck in your teeth.

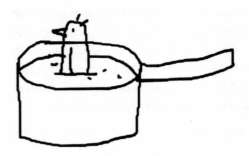

INGREDIENTS

- 3 fruit bats
- 1 tablespoon of finely sliced fresh ginger
- 1 large onion, quartered
- Salt to taste
- Chopped scallions (spring onions)
- Coconut cream and/or soy sauce

METHOD

Wash the bats thoroughly, leaving them intact with their skins on. Place them in a large kettle and add water to cover the ginger, onion and salt. Bring to the boil and cook for 40 minutes. Strain the broth into a second kettle. Skin the bats and throw away the skins. Remove the meat from the bones and return the meat along with any viscera you fancy, to the broth. Heat. Serve liberally sprinkled with scallions (spring onions) and further seasoned with coconut cream and/or soy sauce. Serves four people.

Recipe: *The New York Times Natural Foods Cookbook* by Jean Hewitt, 1971

Scorpion soup

CHINA

If you get stung in a restaurant, it is usually by the bill rather than by your soup. However, the recipe for scorpion soup – a culinary treat in southern China, where it is said to cure rheumatism and even cancer – uses live scorpions, which can give you a nasty nip as you toss them into the wok.

A gentleman by the name of Wing Li from Guangdong was stung three times as he tried to throw his dinner into the pot and ended up in hospital. 'I thought, as they are for eating, they must be harmless,' he complained. 'And it hasn't helped my rheumatism'.

When you bite into the scorpion's abdomen it will explode in your mouth and you will probably need toothpicks to remove the creature's tiny claws from between your teeth. Scorpions have white meat and a woody taste and should be eaten whole except for the tip of the tail. Some recipes say the venom in the tail is rendered harmless by cooking but it's probably wise not to take any chances. Safer still, stick to chicken soup.

INGREDIENTS

- ½ cup of oil
- 30–40 live scorpions
- 125g of fresh pork
- 1 large crushed garlic bulb
- Salt and pepper
- 500ml of water
- Chopped fresh ginger root
- 1 handful of dried Chinese dates
- 1 handful of dried red berries
- 1 large carrot, sliced

METHOD

Heat the oil in a large wok. Wash the scorpions and stir-fry them for 20 seconds. Add the pork, garlic, salt and pepper. Stir-fry briefly, then add the water slowly. Add the other ingredients and simmer on a low heat for 40 minutes. This soup can be eaten either as a starter or as a main course.

Recipe: *entomophagy.wikia.com*

Dried seahorse soup

CHINA

There are some meats that offer endless permutations – rib, leg, rump, loin and so on; one delicious cut after another. Then there is seahorse.

Quite apart from the cute factor, why would anyone want to eat a tiny, bony seahorse? The answer is that, like so many creatures that end up on an Asian menu, it is believed to possess medicinal properties, being particularly beneficial to male sex drive. Rumour has it that a dose of seahorse can cure impotence and premature ejaculation, and if the male seahorse in your soup happens to be pregnant (yes, male seahorses are the ones that carry the eggs), so much the better.

The seahorse has been part of traditional Chinese medicine for centuries, its role as 'sex god' stemming partly from a lifestyle that sees pairs mate for life and produce as many as 1,000 young in the course of a year. Whereas humans produce billions of sperm but only one or two young at a time, seahorses produce a few hundred sperm, but give birth to around 100 in one go. That is some strike rate! No wonder China sells over 20 million farmed seahorses a year in an industry thought to be worth more than $40 million annually. Seahorses may be small but they are big business.

In spite of their supposed attributes, they are certainly not to everyone's taste. Writing on the Asia Obscura website, Andy Deemer described seahorse as 'unbearably salty and fishy. Predictably crunchy, it broke apart quickly, meaning so many more pieces to chew up. I grimaced, but kept chewing, as sharp ends broke apart and found their way trapped between my gums and my lips. It really was quite disgusting.'

Although there is almost ten times more pork in seahorse soup than actual seahorse, there is no escaping the star of the show, simply because, anatomically intact, it is floating there like a baby dragon. Some recipes like to use two seahorses – one male and one female – presumably as a nod to their sexual prowess. Given their lifetime of loyalty and devotion, and that there is no way of knowing whether your meal was ever a couple, it seems to be adding insult to injury to put a pair of complete strangers together. It almost amounts to posthumous infidelity to have the male sleeping with another female in a bowl of soup, especially as in these days of food blogs the pictures of them lying in broth often go all over the internet.

INGREDIENTS
- 45g walnuts
- 4 red dates
- 45g dried seahorse
- 400g lean pork
- 3 pieces of fresh ginger
- salt and pepper

METHOD

Shell and peel the walnuts. Remove the pits of the dates, rinse and soak in water. Soak the dried seahorse in warm water. Rinse the pork. Place all the ingredients in a pot of water, bring it to a rolling boil, then simmer for 2 hours. Season to taste and serve.

Recipe: *learnchineserecipe.com*

Raw blood soup

VIETNAM

___

Tiet canh is a traditional Vietnamese dish of raw blood and cooked meat. It dates back to a time when people used to slaughter ducks, chickens or pigs for worship and then eat the blood and innards. You could also try dog, deer, goose or goat should you have an axe to grind with any of these creatures. Gory to the eye and metallic on the tongue, the dish is rich in protein and is usually served with strong alcohol as an appetizer. The Vietnamese also eat it at breakfast, when it would make a formidable hangover cure.

In 2014, the Vietnamese Minister of Agriculture and Rural Development warned people against eating *tiet canh* amid fears that the raw blood could transmit bird flu. Should you need a reason for not eating raw blood soup, this seems as good as any.

INGREDIENTS
- Duck blood
- Fish sauce
- Duck gizzards
- Peanuts
- Coriander
- Mint
- Water

METHOD

Take one dead duck and hang it so that you can draw its blood into a bowl. Prevent it from coagulating prematurely by mixing it with some fish sauce. The ideal ratio is about four soup spoons of fish sauce to one litre of blood. Boil the chopped duck gizzards in water, and once cooked, place the meat in a shallow dish along with a sprinkling of crushed peanuts and chopped coriander and mint. Add the watery broth in which the duck meat has cooked to the blood and fish sauce mixture in order to encourage coagulation. Quickly pour the blood over the meat. When the blood has set, the result looks like a cross between a pizza with extra tomato and a crime scene. If you are not ready to eat it straight away, you can keep the blood nicely coagulated by cooling the dish in a refrigerator, because if it is left at room temperature the blood will soon return to a liquid state.

Recipe: *www.mycitycuisine.org*

Bird's nest soup

CHINA

When Chinese restaurants first appeared on British high streets, one item on the menu stood out as a symbol of the mysteries of the Orient: bird's nest soup. In the absence of twigs, few believed that it was made from real bird's nests – it was surely nothing more than a fancy name. In many respects it is a fancy name – to disguise the fact that you are drinking what is essentially a bowl of spit.

For the bird's nests in question are all too real and contain the key ingredient of swiftlet saliva, which has dried to act as a cement binding the rest of the nest (seaweed, moss, hair and feathers) to the wall of a cave. The nests are supposedly rich in nutrients and are highly prized because, along with everything from rhinoceros horn to your granny's undies, they are thought to boost libido. They have been used in Chinese cooking for over 400 years and are very expensive, the average nest currently selling for $2,500 per kilo, which makes you wonder whether it really was the genuine article that was served up in Watford High Street in the early 1970s. I do remember seeing a sparrow looking quite forlorn.

When all the swiftlet droppings are washed clean (you know what kids are like), and the nest is boiled and simmered in water for a couple of hours, it acquires a gelatinous texture, which is sometimes thickened by the addition of cornstarch. The taste is unremarkable (the *Independent*'s Graham Hoyland wrote that it tasted like 'a well boiled loofah') and therefore by the standards of this book not overly offensive. However, the fact remains that you have been eating something else's saliva and you should still be left with pangs of guilt for having made a family of small birds homeless.

INGREDIENTS
- 2oz of bird's nest
- 2 slices of fresh ginger
- Salt

METHOD
Soak the bird's nest in cold water overnight. Rinse well and search thoroughly for any feathers and other debris. Boil a pan of water and simmer the bird's nest in it for about 5 minutes. Rinse well and squeeze dry. Boil the nest again in a pan of water with the ginger and salt and simmer for about 2 hours until it is quite soft.

Recipe: *chinesefood.about.com*

Mouse kebabs

MALAWI

If you stop for a roadside snack in Malawi, instead of a McDonald's or a Burger King you are more likely to find a stall selling mouse kebabs – towers of blackened, roasted field mice impaled on sticks. As many as fifteen corpses can fit on a single stick, and lest you should have any doubts as to what you are eating, the vendors kindly leave the head, legs, tail and fur on.

The dish was originally born out of poverty, from the need to utilise anything that was edible and in great supply, but it has subsequently entered mainstream Malawian cuisine. Even those not on the brink of starvation in this poorest of countries happily tuck into a mouse kebab. The locals call it *mbewa*, although the term can refer to any type of rodent, of which there are plenty in Malawi.

Malawians have devised a number of ingenious methods of killing the mice. Following the harvest, when the mice have grown pleasingly plump on a feast of grain and grass, children bludgeon them to death with sticks after setting fires at the entrance to their nests. An alternative method involves digging holes and setting down clay pots filled with water. The mouth of the pot is smeared with corn husks and as the mice seek out the husks, they fall into

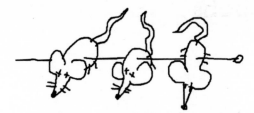

the pot and drown. The children can earn around $2 a day from selling their kebabs, so at least the mice did not die in vain.

These youngsters have become such a part of the country's culture that eight of them even formed their own gospel boy band, the Malawi Mouse Boys, after being discovered by Grammy-winning American record producer Ian Brennan. When Brennan was asked if he would like a taste of their other line of work, he politely declined, saying: 'I am a vegetarian. I have the perfect excuse.'

In fact, there can be few better arguments for turning vegetarian than mouse kebabs.

INGREDIENTS
- 8 field mice
- Salt or cayenne pepper
- 1 sharp, long stick

METHOD
Clean the field mice, thread onto a stick or skewer and roast or grill until tender. Season with salt or cayenne pepper and eat the entire mouse, including the bones.

Recipe: *Daily Mail*

Jellied moose nose

CANADA

So you are standing in your kitchen, sharp knife in hand, with a dead moose lying on the table. Your immediate thought is to discard the less desirable sections so as to reduce the creature to more manageable proportions, but whatever you do, don't throw away the nose. It could prove the major talking point at your next dinner party.

In the remote settlements of northern Canada and Alaska, moose meat is regularly served at social events, where the softest parts of the animal, the liver and the nose, are dished out to village elders. Strange as it may seem, being handed a plate of jellied moose nose is viewed as a compliment, even an honour. The bulbous nose can grow to the size of a volleyball and, once you have plucked out all the hairs, it can be cooked, cooled, sliced and served as a gelatinous cold meat platter with a taste not unlike beef tongue.

In 2009, a reader of *The Times* in England nominated jellied moose nose as the world's worst recipe, having found it in a 1961 cookbook titled *Out of Alaska's Kitchens*. This is a bit harsh, not only because the competition for world's worst recipe is so fierce, but also because, at the very least, the nose looks better on a plate than it does on a moose.

INGREDIENTS

- 1 upper jawbone of a moose, including the nose
- 1 onion, sliced
- 1 garlic clove
- 1 tablespoon of mixed pickling spice
- 1 teaspoon of salt
- ½ teaspoon of pepper
- ¼ cup of vinegar

METHOD

Place the jawbone in a large kettle of hot water and boil for 45 minutes. Remove and chill in cold water. Pull out all the hairs, which will have been loosened by the boiling, and wash thoroughly until there are none left. Place the nose in a kettle and cover with fresh water. Add onion, garlic, spices and vinegar. Bring to a boil, then reduce the heat and simmer until the meat is tender. Allow it to cool overnight in the liquid. When cool, take the meat out of the broth and discard the bones and the cartilage. You will be left with two kinds of meat – white meat from the bulb of the nose and thin strips of dark meat from along the bones and jowls. Slice the meat thinly and alternate layers of white and dark meat. Reheat the broth to boiling, then pour it over the meat. Allow it to cool until the jelly has set. Slice and serve cold.

Recipe: *www.truenorthtimes.ca*

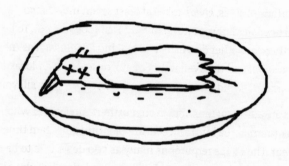

Kiviak

INUIT

The next time anyone in the family complains about having turkey for Christmas, try serving them *kiviak* instead, especially if they have ever hinted at a craving for auk. The good thing about *kiviak* is it does not need cooking, but the downside is that if you think preparing the festive turkey is a laborious process, *kiviak* takes at least seven months, so you will need to start sometime in May. Fast food it is not. To be honest, there are other downsides to making *kiviak*, such as the taste, the smell and the availability of auk or seal in your local supermarket. Oh, and if you get the recipe wrong, it may kill you.

Kiviak is a traditional Inuit dish from northern Greenland where both auk (a small sea bird) and seal are plentiful at certain times of the year. The recipe requires as many as 500 dead auks to be crammed tightly into a rotten old seal skin and placed under a large rock until they have fermented into what has been described as a 'sticky, pungent, toxic, cheesy gloop'. And those in the know say it tastes every bit as good as it sounds. The remaining fat from the seal tenderizes the auk meat, the tastiest part of which is said to be the heart, to the point where the innards become essentially a liquid. Most locals consume their auk by biting off the bird's head and sucking out the juices inside, thereby enjoying a nutritious drink and meal at the same time. With an odour no better or worse than you would expect from a decaying corpse, *kiviak* is best eaten outdoors to prevent the stench filling the home for weeks. Yet repulsive as the dish sounds, it is considered an Inuit delicacy, popular at Christmas, birthdays and weddings, which may explain why Inuit favour long engagements.

In 2013, *kiviak* prompted a food poisoning scare in Siorapaluk after eider ducks were used in the recipe instead of auk. These larger birds did not ferment properly inside the seal, leading to the death of a seventy-one-year-old man from botulism. Alas, oblivious to the fact that the man had not died simply of old age, his friends served the same eider *kiviak* at his funeral as a treat, which ended up killing his daughter and putting five more people into hospital. Others developed such severe hallucinations from the meal that when the helicopter arrived to transport the sick to hospital, they seemed to think they were coming under attack and fired at it with their guns.

In a land where food is scarce in winter, *kiviak* is better than starving, but maybe only just.

INGREDIENTS

- 500 auks
- 1 seal
- 1 dollop of seal grease
- 1 large rock

METHOD

First remove all the flesh from the body of a dead seal. Pack as many auks as possible into the hollowed-out seal carcass. Every part of the auk should be used, including beak, feet and feathers. Press out most of the air from the seal skin, then sew it closed and smear the join with seal grease to repel flies and prevent spoilage. Place a large rock (or several smaller rocks) on top of the carcass to keep the air content low and allow the birds to ferment for at least 7 months. Pluck the feathers, rip off the wings and eat the bird raw, bones and all.

Recipe: *thefourthcontinent.com*

Boiled gannet

WESTERN ISLES

The toughest thing about a gannet is catching the thing in the first place. The birds live high on sheer cliff faces, have beady eyes, sharp beaks and can dive at speeds of over 60 mph. Fortunately for the villagers of Ness on the isle of Lewis in the Western Isles, who have been pursuing the birds for over 500 years, their targets are less mobile baby gannets, or guga as they are known locally. Every August, a team of ten hunters, operating under a special licence, sets off on the six-hour voyage north to Sula Sgeir, a small uninhabited rock with 300-foot-high cliffs. Working in pairs, they spend two weeks living in harsh conditions while killing around 2,000 plump baby gannets. One man snatches the bird from its nest with a rope noose on the end of a long pole before handing it down to his partner who whacks the bird unceremoniously over the head with a stick. The whole business takes about three seconds. The men then singe away the feathers, behead the gannet and remove its wings. It is then stored before being taken back to Ness where it is soaked in brine for around eight weeks.

Those who defend the controversial slaughter point out that the gannet population on the island is booming and that the bird experiences little trauma on its swift journey from nest to catch bag. Indeed some would say that the real trauma is reserved for those who eat it.

One former resident of Lewis described boiled *guga* as 'the most disgusting thing. It's like strong duck stewed in cod liver oil and salt. The taste is bad enough, but my God, the smell as it's boiled! It smells awful, really, really bad, like the worst thing you have ever smelt times 100,000.' Others have labelled it 'revolting and greasy' and with a 'taste somewhere between rotten leather and fishy beef'. Even its fans concede that 'almost nobody outside of Ness can bear the sight of it, the smell of it, and certainly not the taste'. They also advise against eating the skin, which is said to have a 'concentrated flavour and chewy texture not for the fainthearted'. These are not exactly ringing endorsements.

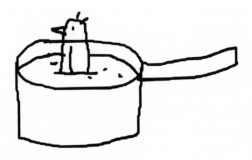

Nevertheless, salted *guga* is exported to New Zealand to satisfy the cravings of exiled Scots, and in 2010 a restaurant in Aberdeen became the first to serve the dish on the UK mainland. There has not exactly been a rush by others wishing to follow suit, possibly because chefs preparing it wear rubber gloves when handling the bird because once its smell is on your skin it is extremely difficult to remove. All things considered, probably the best thing about guga is that it is only available once a year.

INGREDIENTS

- 1 baby gannet
- 1 portion of new potatoes

METHOD

Wash the gannet in cold water and scrub to remove as much grease and salt as possible. There is so much grease that some cooks douse the bird in washing-up liquid. Bring to the boil in clean water. After the first boiling, strain off the excess grease, refill the pan with cold water and then boil again. Continue this process for up to 90 minutes until there is no more grease. *Guga* is customarily served with new potatoes.

Recipe: *The Guardian*

Boiled flamingo

ANCIENT ROME

It would be fair to say that the Romans liked their food. Indeed one emperor, Vitellius, liked it so much that he would stick a feather down his throat between banquet courses so that he could vomit the food up and start eating afresh. Described as a very tall man with a 'vast belly', Vitellius had an appetite that made Henry VIII look positively anorexic. He would eat three or four large meals a day, usually followed by a wild drinks party. These parties were held at a different house each night, the news that Vitellius had invited himself round for supper being enough to send any host into a state of panic.

The Romans enjoyed a varied diet featuring many foods familiar to us today, including tuna, mussels, lamb, pork, plums, pears, tangerines and mushrooms. The basic diet for poorer Romans was equally unremarkable, consisting primarily of pottage, a cereal-based dish made from wheat, corn or millet. It was the porridge of its day. However it was at banquets that the Roman taste for the exotic really came to the fore, with hosts trying to outdo each other by introducing increasingly elaborate dishes. On such occasions it was not unusual to taste heron, dolphin meatballs and ostrich brains. One of the most popular items on the banquet menu was flamingo, although it has to be said that you would probably count yourself unlucky if you got the leg.

If by some misfortune your butcher has run out of flamingo, don't worry. The recipe works just as well with parrot.

INGREDIENTS
- 1 flamingo
- Salt
- Dill
- Vinegar
- Leeks
- Grape juice
- Pepper
- Mint
- Flour

Wash the flamingo and remove the feathers, beak and any other part you do not want to eat. You may choose to lop off the legs, not least because you would struggle to find a cooking vessel big enough to hold them. Truss it firmly so that it retains its shape. Parboil the flamingo in a large saucepan of water with salt, dill and a little vinegar. Next, add a bunch of leeks and coriander. Thicken some grape juice by heating it up and then mix that into the pan. Cover the pan and continue cooking the bird until the flesh is tender. In a separate bowl, crush some pepper, coriander and mint, drizzle them in vinegar and add some of the juice from the saucepan. Stir the sauce and allow to simmer on a low heat. Add flour and cook until the sauce has thickened. When the flamingo is finally cooked, strain the sauce and pour it over the bird.

Recipe: *Cooking and Dining in Imperial Rome* by Apicius

Parrot pie

19TH-CENTURY AUSTRALIA

When it comes to putting food on the table in impoverished times, people have to make do with whatever they can readily catch – and in nineteenth-century Australia parakeet fitted the bill. In the 1820s, the birds were sold for about sixpence each in Sydney markets, or a dozen for a shilling if they were to be baked into a pie. The colourful little parrots landed on so many dinner tables during this period, not only in the remote outback but also in cities, that Mrs. Beeton included a recipe for parrot pie in her *Book of Household Management*, a copy of which was required reading for the aspiring Victorian British housewife.

Mrs. Beeton's recipe below recommends using the entire bird (presumably once it has been beheaded) but other recipes from the same period state that only the breast and thigh meat should go into the pie, the rest of the carcass being used to flavour the stock.

While some early Australian settlers praised parrot pie, for many the bird was eaten more out of necessity than desire, as was its close relative, cockatoo soup. Another variation on the theme, parrot stew, actually became something of an Aussie joke, the recipe being along the lines of: 'Take a parrot and an axe-head, boil them until the axe-head is tender, throw the parrot away and eat the axe-head.'

Parrot pie still appeared occasionally on Australian home menus in the early part of the twentieth century. Recalling her childhood on Fraser Island, where her father was the lighthouse keeper and the supply boat arrived only once a month, Jessie Wadsworth told Woman's Weekly that 'as there was plenty of bird life and wallabies on the island we could always manage with a pigeon or parrot pie or roast wallaby'.

It will come as no surprise to learn that the Romans had a favourite parrot dish – parrot tongue, which was ripped out and served before you could say, 'Who's a pretty boy then?'

INGREDIENTS
- 12 parakeets
- 6 thin slices of lean beef
- 3 hard-boiled eggs
- ½ teaspoon of finely chopped parsley
- Finely grated lemon peel
- Salt and pepper
- Flour
- 4 rashers of bacon
- Stock
- Puff pastry

METHOD

Prepare the birds by trussing them like quail. Line a pie dish with the sliced beef and cover the strips with six of the parakeets. Fill the spaces with sliced egg, parsley and lemon peel, sprinkle with seasoning and coat lightly with flour. On the next layer place the bacon rashers covered by the remaining six parakeets. Again fill the spaces with egg, parsley and lemon and dust with seasoning. Pour in stock or water so that the dish is three-quarters full, cover with puff pastry and bake for about 2 hours. The dish should be enough to feed twelve people, meaning that everyone gets their own parakeet.

Recipe: *www.recipesource.com*

Stuffed thrush

ANCIENT ROME

As we have seen with larks' tongues, the Romans had no qualms about eating songbirds. *Cooking and Dining in Imperial Rome,* by Apicius, lists a recipe for stuffed thrush, a dish that was reputed to cure all manner of stomach complaints. Given the size of the average Roman appetite compared to the size of the average thrush, they would probably have reckoned on a serving of at least three birds per person.

Thrush also features in a thirteenth-century Spanish recipe book describing a dish deemed fit for a king. The compiler wrote: 'One takes a fat young sheep ... and puts [in] a stuffed goose and in the goose's belly a stuffed hen, and in the hen's belly a stuffed young pigeon, and in the pigeon's belly a stuffed thrush and in the thrush's belly another stuffed or fried bird, all of this stuffed and sprinkled with sauce.' It is even suggested that after all that, the sheep should be stuffed inside a calf. It all makes the Aldi four-bird roast sound rather tame.

INGREDIENTS

- 1 song thrush
- Crushed pepper
- ½ cup of juniper berries
- Dill
- Salt
- Leek heads
- Cooking oil

METHOD

Remove the feathers, head, wings, tail and entrails of the thrush and stuff the bird through the throat with a mixture of crushed pepper and juniper berries. Tie the bird tightly with string.

Add the dill, salt and leek heads to a little cooking oil and heat in a frying pan. Place the thrush in the hot oil mixture and fry until golden brown.

Recipe: *Cooking and Dining in Imperial Rome* by Apicius

Roast heron in chaudon sauce

MEDIEVAL ENGLAND

Heron was widely eaten in medieval times, possibly because of a superstition held at the time that the fat of a heron killed at full moon would cure rheumatism.
The English roasted it with ginger, the Italians cooked it with garlic and onions, the Germans and Dutch made it into pies, and the French liked to decorate the serving platter with flowers to make it look more appealing. In most cases the heron's head was first tucked under its wing so that it would fit into an oven.

As late as 1914, a recipe for heron pudding appeared in *The British Home Cookery Book* by May Byron. In it, she warned of the perils of breaking the heron's bones before cooking. 'These bones are filled with a fishy fluid, which, if allowed to come in contact with the flesh, makes the whole bird taste of fish.'

Heron was often used as a substitute for swan, goose or peacock. The recipe below for roast heron dates back to fourteenth-century England and uses the bird's blood to beef up the sauce. Obviously aware that this might be too extreme even in an age when you could be boiled in oil, have your eyes burned out and fingers torn off for committing forgery, the writer suggests that you might prefer to replace the blood with toasted breadcrumbs.

INGREDIENTS
- 1 heron
- Olive oil
- Salt
- Broth
- Ginger
- Galingale
- Red wine vinegar

METHOD

Clean and gut the heron and put the giblets to one side. Coat the bird's exterior with olive oil and roast on a spit or in an oven, basting from time to time. Meanwhile wash the blood from the giblets into a bowl and while still wet sprinkle them with a little salt. Put the salted giblets into a pot, cover them with water and boil them until they are cooked. Remove the giblets, drain them and allow to cool. Chop the giblets into small pieces and mix into the broth with the powdered spices and heron blood (for colour) to create a gravy-like chaudon sauce. Add salt and then bring to the boil before reducing to a simmer and adding a little vinegar. Serve the sauce with the roasted heron.

Recipe: *www.godecookery.com*

Sheep's head

NORWAY

___

Sheep's head, or *smalahove*, is a traditional main course in western Norway, originally served with sour milk or beer. It used to be a staple diet of the poor, arising from the need not to waste any part of the animal, but today it is considered a delicacy on special occasions – especially around Christmas – as well as something of a tourist attraction. The town of Voss, in particular, has built up a thriving trade from visitors keen to try *smalahove*, partly because it is an authentic rural Norwegian dish but more importantly because it represents another box ticked in their quest to sample the world's most extreme foods. And when you look down at a sheep's head lying motionless on your plate next to a portion of boiled potatoes and mashed swede, it is something you are only likely to experience again in nightmares.

In truth, these days *smalahove* will almost certainly be composed of the head of a lamb rather than an adult sheep, following a 1998 European Union directive to combat the possible transmission of the disease scrapie.

Before cooking, the head is salted, sometimes smoked and dried. The animal's brain is usually removed before salting but it can be cooked inside the skull and eaten by scooping it out with a spoon. A serving generally consists of half a head, which has the advantage of allowing it to lie flat on the plate with just one eye looking up at you pitifully. The areas around the ear and eye are normally eaten first as they are the fattiest and are best eaten warm. The standard practice is to eat the head from front to back, beginning by cutting between the teeth in the upper and lower jaw. The jaw is then ripped open to allow easy access to the eye. Along with the eye muscle, the tongue is reputed to be the tastiest part. The meat with the least fat can be found in the area around the jaw.

If you are in a large party all having *smalahove* at Christmas, an entertaining diversion before tucking in to your meal could be to try and pair up the half-heads to see if any couple at the table has the same animal. Or you could just pull a cracker.

INGREDIENTS
- 1 lamb's head (serves 2 people)
- 6 litres of water
- 3lb of salt
- 1 cup of sugar
- 1 sharp axe

METHOD

Burn the skin and fleece from the lamb's head. Cut the skull in half lengthways with an axe, remove the brain if required and soak the remaining head in cold water for at least 24 hours, changing the water several times. Dry the head thoroughly and then make brine from the mixture of water, salt and sugar. Soak the half-head in the brine for three days. Then smoke over fresh juniper, dry oak or alder before leaving to dry for up to 6 months. On the day of the feast, boil or steam the head in water for around 3 hours until the meat loosens from the cheek bones and serve with vegetables.

Recipe: *www.matoppskrift.no*

Yak penis

CHINA

___

You haven't lived until you have had penis in your mouth. This is pretty much the sales pitch of the Guolizhuang restaurant in Beijing that specializes in serving animal penises – including water buffalo, deer, horse, donkey, goat, dog, snake, seal, duck and yak. Of these, yak is believed to be the most nutritious. At around $220 it is certainly among the most expensive, but you do get a lot for your money. If served uncut, it coils around the plate like a young python and extends for more inches than any man would care to contemplate. A meal of yak penis not only leaves you feeling full but also inadequate. Equally, if it is served already chopped into smaller bite-sized pieces you feel the yak's pain.

Young people under the age of fifteen are not allowed to eat in the restaurant for fear that the hormones in the food will interfere with natural growth. Similarly the establishment's waiters advise women customers against eating testicles (you see, it is not a members-only restaurant – there is something else on the menu for those who don't fancy penis) because the hormones might give them deeper voices and beards.

Yak penis was first mentioned in China's *Records of Renowned Doctors* from AD520. As well as being rich in protein and good for the skin, it was inevitably thought to enhance virility and was prescribed to old men who had lost their sexual vigour. It was the Viagra of its day. It can be served in a variety of ways – cooked in hot chilli oil, grilled and inserted into a hollowed-out melon or simply roasted and laid to rest proudly on a bed of lettuce. As the size of the average yak member would put a male porn star to shame, it is a dish best shared.

It can also be made into a hearty soup. If you think yak penis soup is too revolting for words, remember that the next time you open a can of oxtail. Which would you rather eat, the animal's pride and joy or the body part that has spent all year swatting flies away from its arse?

INGREDIENTS FOR YAK PENIS SOUP
- 1 yak penis
- A little ginger
- A little Sichuan pepper
- ½ cup of rice wine
- ½ cup of wolfberries

METHOD

Peel off the outer skin of the penis and cut it in half lengthwise along the urethra. Clean and soak in cold water for 30 minutes. Place the penis in a large pan of water and bring to the boil. Skim any fat from the surface of the liquid and then add the ginger, pepper and wine. Cook slowly over a low heat for about 3 hours and then strain off the spices. Bring back to the boil and continue to simmer on low heat for another 3 hours. When the penis is almost cooked, remove it and cut into bite-sized pieces. Return the segments to the pan, add the wolfberries, bring back to the boil and simmer until tender. The entire cooking process takes around 10 hours.

Recipe: *www.seriouseats.com*

Roast guinea pig

PERU

Kept as a pet in many parts of the world, the guinea pig leads a markedly less pampered existence in the Andes mountains, where, instead of being required to do nothing more than look fluffy and scamper around a cage, it is raised commercially in readiness for the cooking pot. Consequently, any guinea pig about to be adopted is strongly advised to check first whether its prospective new owner has a South American passport. It really is a matter of life and death.

In Andean cuisine the guinea pig is known as *cuy* on account of the sound it makes. Guinea pig has been a food source for over 5,000 years. In the days of the Incas it was consumed solely by the nobility or used as a means of foretelling the future via its entrails – a gory version of reding your tea leaves. A thousand white guinea pigs were sacrificed each year in Cusco's main square to placate the gods and ensure a bountiful crop harvest. The animal's significance is such that Peruvian-influenced depictions of Christ's Last Supper show the twelve disciples tucking into a meal of guinea pig.

Guinea pig, was also used in ancient medicine. Folk doctors called *curanderos* would rub a guinea pig over a sick patient's body in the belief that the animal would squeak when it passed over an affected area. Black guinea pigs were said to be particularly adept at this procedure. It seems that people were happy to put their faith in Dr. Cuy.

The tastiest parts of the guinea pig are the nose, ears and little hands, the overall flavour a cross between rabbit and pork. It is served in different ways in different regions – roasted, grilled, fried or baked. Some restaurants are dedicated solely to guinea pig while leading chefs have started treating it as a gourmet item, serving it as a terrine or instead of smoked fish in Peruvian-Japanese *Nikkei* dishes. The flavour changes slightly according to the animal's colour, the ones with multi-coloured fur being considered the best.

In total, an estimated 65 million guinea pigs are eaten each year in Peru alone. The guinea pig keeps the production line ticking along nicely by reproducing much quicker than cows or pigs. Guinea pigs take up less room than traditional livestock and are cheaper to feed. Their meat is high in protein and low in cholesterol and fat. They can be bought in markets, already skinned and cleaned, and are usually split apart and cooked whole with the head, teeth and ears left intact. If you prefer to leave the skin on, smear it with salt so that it crisps up. As an added ignominy in the Cusco region of Peru it is treated as a small suckling pig and cooked with a hot pepper in its mouth.

Guinea pigs are considered so important to Peruvian society that in many towns they are honoured with annual festivals, at which they are pampered, dressed up in cute little outfits and then eaten. There is no room for sentiment. They also have their own national holiday, Guinea Pig Day, on the second Friday of October. Quite what they do on their day off is unclear.

INGREDIENTS

- 2 guinea pigs
- 2 red onions
- 4 cloves of garlic
- 2 teaspoons of cumin
- 1 teaspoon of white pepper
- 2 teaspoons of salt
- 2 tablespoons of water
- 2 tablespoons of oil
- 2 tablespoons of lard

METHOD

Skin the guinea pig in hot water, open near its abdomen, remove the organs and intestines and cleanse well in salted water. Hang the guinea pig carcass to drain and dry. Mix together all the remaining ingredients apart from the lard and spread over the inside and outside of the guinea pig. Allow to marinate for one day. Before roasting, remove excess marinade to avoid scalding. Insert the spit into the back part of the animal and exit from the jaw. Once it is on the stick, tie its front and back feet, stretching out the legs. Put on the grill, turning manually. Apply lard to the skin to prevent it drying out. The guinea pig is ready to be served when its skin is close to bursting, meaning that leaving it to cook for too long could prove distressing for all present. It can be served in a spicy sauce with rice or potatoes.

Recipe: *wikipedia*

Fried beaver tail

NORTH AMERICA

If you see beaver tails in a shop in Canada these days, the chances are that they will be flat pastries sold under that trade name. However, a few inventive cooks do fry real beaver tails and smoke and boil the rest of the beaver for another nourishing meal. The recipe below appeared in a wonderful 1967 book titled *Northern Cookbook*, which also gives instructions on how to prepare such wilderness gems as boiled lynx, stuffed muskrat and baked skunk. The author helpfully points out that the last-named tastes like rabbit and has no smell when cooked. Skunk fat was also said to be a cure for whooping cough.

Although very much a rarity these days on the North American dinner table, fried beaver tail is still considered a delicacy in some quarters, due to its large fat content. Beaver tail also makes a nourishing soup and can even be pickled as a true gourmet treat. Apparently the flavour of young beaver meat is not unlike goose, although others have compared the taste to pork.

Before you turn your nose up at the thought of eating beaver tail, it might be worth remembering that you may well have sampled beaver anus. Castoreum, the substance emitted from the castor sacs within the beaver's butt, is occasionally used as a natural food flavouring, in place of vanilla. It is also more commonly used in the perfume industry to replicate the smell of leather. And to think all the beaver does with it is use it to mark its territory.

INGREDIENTS

- 2 beaver tails
- ½ cup of vinegar
- 1 tablespoon of salt
- 2 teaspoons of soda
- ¼ cup of flour
- ¼ teaspoon of pepper
- ¼ cup of butter
- ¼ cup of sherry or cooking wine
- 1 teaspoon of dry mustard
- 1 teaspoon of sugar
- 1 tablespoon of Worcestershire sauce

METHOD

Skin the beaver tails, clean them thoroughly and wash well in a solution of salt water. Allow them to soak overnight in cold water, adding half a cup of vinegar and a tablespoon of salt to the water. The next day, remove the tails from the brine, wash them again and then cover them with a solution of two teaspoons of soda to two quarts of water. Bring to a boil, reduce the heat and simmer for 10 minutes. Drain then dredge the beaver tails in seasoned flour. Melt the butter in a large frying pan and sauté the tails at a low heat until they are tender. Mix the wine with the mustard, sugar and Worcestershire sauce. Add the mix to the beaver tails and simmer gently for 10 minutes, basting frequently.

Recipe: *Northern Cookbook*, edited by Eleanor A. Ellis, 1967

Boiled cow's womb

ROMAN

Few of us have knowingly eaten an animal's womb, but let's be honest, you can never be too sure what goes into some processed meats. The Romans were happy to eat any body part, so they harvested wombs from sterile cows and treated them as sausage casings by filling them with a mix of ground meat, leeks and nuts and then boiling them. As an alternative recipe, they would grill the womb and serve it in a spicy sauce.

Apparently the uterus itself does not possess much flavour, which was why the Romans chose to stuff it with stronger ingredients, but it is believed to impart some sort of youthful, feminine energy to the eater. On the downside, it has been described as smelling of 'very wet dog', rarely an odour that is willingly introduced to the kitchen.

INGREDIENTS

- Crushed pepper
- Cumin
- Leeks
- Ground meat
- Pine nuts
- 1 cow's womb
- Dill

METHOD

Crush pepper and cumin with two small heads of peeled leek. Add the ground meat and pine nuts and stuff the mixture into the cow's womb. Boil in water with a bunch of leeks and dill.

Recipe: *Cooking and Dining in Imperial Rome* by Apicius

Roasted cow's udder

SEVENTEENTH-CENTURY ENGLAND

Faced with a cow's udder for the first time, cooks could be forgiven for not knowing whether to serve it with vegetables or a tennis racket. Or try to get a tune out of it. Yet it has featured sporadically in recipes across the world for 350 years.

Opinion was divided among early English chroniclers regarding the merits of cow's udder. Samuel Pepys wrote in his diary: 'Mr Creed and I to the Leg in King Street, where he and I, and my Will, had a good udder to dinner.' However a century later, Parson James Woodforde was less complimentary, writing in his diary for 17 February, 1763: 'I dined at the Chaplain's table with Pickering and Waring, upon a roasted Tongue and Udder ... N.B. I shall not dine on a roasted Tongue and Udder again soon.' Since the cleric continued to eat tongue regularly over the next forty years, it is fair to assume that it was the udder that offended his taste buds.

Boiling a cow's udder so that the meat was tenderized could take an entire day in Stuart or Hanoverian kitchens. Udder could be served hot or cold or as a pie filling along with cock's combs. Cold udder was still being served in parts of the UK as recently as the 1970s. Cooked in milk, sliced and put in a sandwich, it was seen as an alternative to luncheon meat with its soft texture and sweet flavour. Although it seems to have become extinct from British and US kitchens due to food safety concerns, pre-cooked udder remains a popular delicacy in the street markets of Florence and it can occasionally be found pot-roasted in France or fried in a schnitzel in parts of Germany. The recipe below first appeared in a 1615 publication *Countrey* (sic) *Contentments* by Gervase Markham.

INGREDIENTS

- 1 cow's udder
- Cloves
- Butter
- Vinegar
- White breadcrumbs
- Sugar
- Cinnamon

METHOD

Take a washed cow's udder and boil it until tender. Allow to cool. Cover the udder with cloves, then roast until brown, basting it with butter from time to time. Boil vinegar, butter and white breadcrumbs so that the mixture thickens and then sprinkle with sugar and cinnamon. Lay the mix in a clean dish, add the udder so that it is coated with the breadcrumb mix and serve.

Recipe: *www.theoldfoodie.com*

Dormouse stew

SLOVENIA

The edible dormouse (or *glis glis*) has been an ingredient in Slovenian cuisine for over 500 years, its fate sealed at birth by the misfortune of being saddled with the prefix 'edible'. In his travel diary of the 1480s, priest Paolo Santonino wrote of a lunch stop at a household in Inner Carniola (part of modern-day Slovenia) where the farmer's wife hastily prepared a roast dormouse for the hungry archbishop.

The dormouse was dealt another bum hand by the authors of Slovenian legend who claim that the little creature is possessed by the devil himself and therefore fully deserves to be hunted, killed and tossed into the stewing pot at the first available opportunity. Slovenians seem to have a love-hate relationship with the creature because you can visit a museum dedicated to the dormouse in Cerknica and celebrate Dormouse Night every October. The fact that this takes place at the height of the hunting season must take some of the shine off the celebration for the dormouse. In fairness, the dormouse has not helped its own cause by its sheer stupidity. Operating under the cover of darkness, it should be able to forage in safety but instead persists in emitting frequent high-pitched squeaks which inevitably attract hunters with flashlights. Short of wearing a fluorescent jacket and yelling 'I'm over here', it couldn't make its presence much more obvious.

The dormouse was not only hunted for its food, but also for its fur. Reasoning that it would require a hell of a lot of dormouse pelts to make a decent-sized coat, manufacturers focused instead on more achievable goals and the dormouse fur hat became a Slovenian fashion statement from the late eighteenth century. It takes about thirty-six pelts to make a hat with ear-flaps.

Dormouse fat was also considered to have medicinal properties and was used for curing broken bones, bruises, upset stomachs and rheumatism, even though about ten large dormice were needed to obtain half a litre of fat. Modern Slovenians use the fat to oil machinery.

Up until World War II, Slovenians smoked dormouse meat as an alternative to ham while the liver was considered a real delicacy. Today, Slovenia's favourite dormouse dish is *polšja obara*, or dormouse stew, but it can also be used in soups, risottos and goulashes. The little dormouse is simply too versatile for its own good.

The Romans were also fond of eating stuffed dormouse. They used to keep the rodents in terracotta jars with a ready supply of walnuts, chestnuts and acorns. The dormice, having thought they had landed in paradise, stuffed themselves to twice their normal size, at which point they discovered that they were bound instead for the roasting pot. The Romans liked to serve them dipped in honey or stuffed with a mixture of pork and pine nuts.

Dormouse connoisseurs say it has a strong smell and a gamey flavour. At least it doesn't taste like chicken.

INGREDIENTS

- 4 dormice
- 4 tablespoons of butter or oil
- ½ cup of all-purpose flour
- 1lb of potatoes, peeled and cubed
- 1 teaspoon of salt
- 2 tablespoons of chopped fresh parsley
- 2 tablespoons of fresh marjoram
- 2 or 3 peppercorns
- Grated peel of 1 lemon
- 1 tablespoon of vinegar

Cut the dormouse meat into medium-sized pieces. Heat the butter or oil in a large skillet. Fry the meat over medium to high heat for 10 to 12 minutes or until the meat is browned. Add the flour and stir. Continue to cook over medium heat for another 3 to 4 minutes. Add enough water to the pan to cover the meat. Add the potatoes, salt, parsley, marjoram, peppercorns and lemon peel. Cover and cook over medium heat for about 30 minutes. The stew is ready when the potatoes and meat are tender. Add the vinegar and stir. Serves four people.

Recipe: *Flavors of Slovenia: Food and Wine from Central Europe's Hidden Gem* by Heike Milhench, 2007

Badger stew

ROADKILL

Do you ever get tired of pre-packed supermarket meat? Why not try roadkill instead? It's organic, it's free, the potential choice is extensive, and once you've removed the flies and dried blood, it's ready to cook. If you're really lucky with your choice of dead animal, there might even be some tyre marks on the body to create that nice griddle effect.

A restaurant in Darwin, Australia, specializes in roadkill dishes, using the motto: 'You kill it, we grill it'. Crocodile is a particular favourite on the menu, and guess what, it tastes like chicken.

Arthur Boyt from Cornwall has been eating roadkill since the 1960s – from dogs and cats to polecats and mice – and thinks more people should follow his example. His favourite is dog, and he has eaten two lurchers and a Labrador which were hit by cars. He tried unsuccessfully to contact the owners before putting the animals in the freezer. He compared the 'smooth, round, sweet' flavour of dog meat to lamb, adding: 'I'd drink a red wine with it – possibly a Chianti'.

'I've never been ill from eating roadkill,' he said. 'People have been here for a meal and been sick when they got home – but I'm sure that was something else.'

A fellow devotee, Jonathan McGowan, a naturalist and taxidermist from Bournemouth, has lived on roadkill for over thirty years ever since he found and cooked a dead adder when he was fourteen. Shunning the supermarket, he has instead dined on moles, mice, hedgehogs, badgers, gulls, crows, owls, stoats, blackbirds, rats, squirrels and anything else he can find on the highways and byways of Britain.

Owl curry and badger stew (recipe below) are among his signature dishes, while another of his specialities is pan-fried crane flies, served with olive oil, celery and raisins. 'It's a bit like a Waldorf salad,' he told the *Daily Mail*, 'only with daddy longlegs. I don't eat the legs though; that would be weird'.

He says adder tastes a bit like bacon rind, foxes are delicious and lean, rats are like pork but salty, and squirrels have good firm white meat similar to rabbit and with a distinctly nutty flavour. He is less keen on mice and hedgehogs, the latter being very fatty, but reserves his strongest condemnation for moles. 'They are horrible and have a rancid taste,' he admits. 'They have an unpleasant taste in their skin to ward off predators. Wild animals don't eat them. I've only had one once and never again.'

INGREDIENTS

- 1 badger
- 100g of butter
- 1 glass of Armagnac
- 1 bottle of dry, sparkling wine
- 1 glass of pig's blood
- 2 egg yolks
- 1 pot of crème fraîche
- 500g of wild mushrooms or chestnuts

METHOD

Skin the badger, remove its entrails and soak it in water, ideally a fast-flowing river, for at least 48 hours. This will help you to de-grease the animal. Once the badger is de-greased, remove its liver. Cut the rest of the flesh into pieces and brown them in a frying pan with butter until the chunks of meat are golden and stiff. Flambé with a glass of Armagnac and pour in the bottle of wine. Simmer gently for 2 hours before adding the chopped badger liver (cooked previously in a little oil), the pig's blood, the egg yolks and crème fraîche and serve immediately with either wild mushrooms or chestnuts. The stew serves four people.

Recipe: *Daily Mail*

Hedgehog spaghetti carbonara

ROADKILL

Everybody loves cute little hedgehogs, so the thought of killing and cooking them is too hideous for most of us to contemplate. Yet roasted hedgehog was one of the earliest known dishes in Ancient Britain, with evidence that it was eaten over 8,000 years ago. It was as popular a dish in Britain then as roast beef is now. The method of preparation was particularly brutal. Once caught, the hedgehog should have its throat cut before being singed and gutted. If the animal refused to unroll, it was suggested that it be dropped in hot water, whereupon it would obligingly straighten out. It was then trussed like a pullet and cooked for about two hours wrapped in a casing of grass or leaves to stop the meat burning. It was a forerunner of beef wellington.

Happily, hedgehog has long since died out of mainstream cuisine, but it remains a popular roadkill ingredient, not least because its persistent inability to master the most basic of road safety skills means that it is always in plentiful supply on a highway near you. So if you can bear devouring a close relative of Sonic, here is a recipe for hedgehog spaghetti carbonara.

INGREDIENTS
- 250g of lean hedgehog
- 4 eggs
- 60ml of double cream
- 100g of grated parmesan cheese
- 500g of spaghetti
- 1 medium onion (chopped)
- 30ml of olive oil
- 60ml of dry white wine

METHOD

Prise your hedgehog from the road tarmac. After thoroughly cleaning the hedgehog to remove any traces of white lines, skin it and chop the meat into small chunks. Beat the eggs and cream together in a bowl. Add half the parmesan cheese. Put the pasta in boiling water. Put the onions and hedgehog chunks in a pan with olive oil on medium heat until the onions are almost clear. Add the wine and reduce the heat. Drain the pasta when cooked and combine it with the egg, cream and cheese mix. Add the meat, onions and wine and mix thoroughly. Garnish with remaining parmesan.

Recipe: *Daily Telegraph*

Escamoles

Native to Mexico, the Liometopum ant is not an insect to be messed with. It is big, aggressive to the point of being psychopathic and has a venomous bite. So collecting its eggs for the Mexican dish *escamoles* is not a task to be undertaken lightly. It is because of the risks involved in gathering the eggs and their scarcity (they can only be obtained in March and April and even then the nests are sometimes destroyed by rainstorms) that they are highly prized and expensive, costing up to $100 per kilo. Indeed they are often referred to as Mexican caviar.

The eggs and larvae of the ant can be eaten raw and are recommended as survival food should you ever become lost in the Mexican wilderness. In times of emergency, when food supplies are short, you will eat just about anything. After all, millions of Allied soldiers ate Spam during World War II.

Escamoles have been part of Mexican cuisine since the days of the Aztecs. They have a buttery, nutty taste and a texture like cottage cheese. In restaurants, they are often fried and wrapped in tortillas and because their taste is not something that will have you reaching for the sick bucket, it is quite possible that you will have no idea that you have just eaten ant eggs. They could easily be mistaken for fat grains of rice, which makes you wonder why they don't just serve rice in the first place. It's a lot cheaper.

The upshot is that if you go to Mexico and only want to learn one word of the native language, forget about 'hello', 'thank you' and 'the bill'; just remember what escamoles really are.

INGREDIENTS

- 2 cups of *escamoles*
- Cooking oil
- 2 cloves of garlic
- Zest and juice of a lemon
- Half a finely chopped onion
- 1 cup of guacamole
- Tortillas

METHOD

Wash the ant eggs thoroughly in warm water and dry them. Heat cooking oil in a frying pan and add the ant eggs, garlic, lemon, chopped onion and guacamole. Fry well and serve on tortillas. You could also add chilli sauce to the dish and even some grasshoppers for an extra kick.

Recipe: *www.alwaysfoodie.com*

Stir-fried cockroach

CHINA

Cockroaches are probably the last things you want to see in your kitchen, but in the kitchens of northern China the insects are commonplace, albeit usually dead, covered in chilli sauce and lying in a wok.

As China looks for new, cheaper medicines for its ageing population, the country has taken to cockroach farming in a big way. A single farm can rear over 20 million cockroaches, all headed for the pharmaceutical industry, ever since the cockroach was acclaimed as a miracle drug. Creams made from cockroaches are used in Chinese hospitals and the insects are also ground into pills to treat a range of ailments. Therefore it follows that eating the insects should also be beneficial. Claims have been made that eating cockroaches can help to remedy blood clots, gastroenteritis, heart disease and tuberculosis as well as providing a high-protein meal.

When a customer at a restaurant in Chengdu recently had the temerity to complain about finding a dead cockroach in his salad, the waitress said it was perfectly normal and then, to prove her point, she promptly swallowed it.

The secret of a good cockroach is to fry it twice. The second frying makes the shell crispy and the inside succulent with a texture resembling cottage cheese. They can also be grilled, sautéed or boiled, and the Madagascar Hissing Cockroach apparently has a taste and texture like greasy chicken. If you're put off by the thought of devouring a hissing cockroach, remember that all cockroaches tend to hiss when they come into contact with hot cooking oil. Besides, anything that can survive with its head cut off for a month is a food that demands to be taken seriously.

INGREDIENTS

- 5 cockroaches
- 4 tablespoons of cooking oil
- 1 red pepper
- 1 tablespoon of corn starch
- 1 onion
- 1 green pepper
- 1 tablespoon of salt
- 2 cups of rice

METHOD

Remove and discard the solid wing-covering flaps and all the legs of the cockroaches. Put the whole cockroaches into a pot of boiling oil and fry quickly for 15 seconds. Heat a wok until hot. Add four spoons of oil, put all of the vegetables into it and stir-fry for 3 minutes. Put the half-cooked cockroaches into the wok and add salt and cornstarch. Fry quickly again and serve on a bed of white rice.

Recipe: *jamaica-gleaner.com*

Roast cat

MEDIEVAL EUROPE

Feral cats were a major nuisance in the cities of Medieval Europe, so the authorities decided that the best solution to the problem was to eat them. Obviously if a cat was to feed a family of six, you wouldn't want one that was all skin and bones from scouring the streets for scraps. So the search was always on for the plumpest cat available, ideally one fattened up on a steady diet of rats. In those days cats were widely associated with witchcraft, prompting a recipe from the period (see below) to call for the cat to be decapitated and the head thrown away before preparation for the spit as 'eating the brains will cause him who eats them to lose his senses and judgement'. It is easy to see how that might be a cause for concern.

Cat was still occasionally eaten in rural Italy during World War II, and as recently as 2010 veteran Italian TV chef Beppe Bigazzi was dropped by the country's state-owned broadcaster RAI for sharing a recipe for cat stew with horrified viewers. He told them that he had dined on cat many times and that the meat tasted better than chicken or rabbit, adding that in some towns it was nicknamed 'the rabbit that runs on roofs'. Digging himself into an even deeper hole, he informed viewers of an old Tuscan saying: 'If you don't have meat, kill the cat'.

Capitalizing on the pro-feline backlash, a volunteer at Rome's famous Cat Sanctuary, which cares for some 200 feral cats, reminded the public that the cats there were available for adoption 'but not to anyone who arrives here with a cooking pan'.

INGREDIENTS

- 1 fat cat (dead)
- 2 pints of olive oil
- 4 garlic cloves, crushed
- ½ cup of broth

METHOD

Remove the cat's head, slit the body open and take out the entrails. Clean the body inside and out. Wrap the corpse in a clean linen cloth and bury the animal underground for one day and one night. Dig it up and then place it on a spit over a hot fire, greasing the meat with the olive oil and two of the crushed garlic cloves. While it is roasting, continue basting and also whip it repeatedly with a green twig. This must be done before it is well roasted. Don't ask why. When it is finally roasted, the cat can be served on a large plate and drizzled with a thin broth mixed with half a cup of olive oil and the remaining two crushed garlic cloves.

Recipe: *medievalcookery.com*

Grilled lizard

ARABIAN PENINSULA

___

The uromastyx, or spiny-tailed lizard, can grow up to three feet long, making it an ample meal on the Arabian peninsula, where it is popularly known as *soosmar*.
It lives in a sandy burrow and is caught in the spring by hunters using hooks and sometimes sniffer dogs. Apparently the thrill of the chase, which ends with the hunter gleefully jumping on the lizard's back before killing, skinning and gutting it, is surpassed only by its taste, said to resemble, uh, chicken. Confusingly the hunters call it the 'fish of the desert'.

Soosmar is usually grilled and served with rice but it can also be eaten raw, as the locals believe that its blood is an aphrodisiac and that its body fat can cure arthritis. The lizard is in ready supply partly because it is not particularly bright. After cleaners in the city of Ar Rass found a uromastyx in a cemetery, they were wheeling it through the streets when it escaped and headed straight for the nearest restaurant, attracted by the smell of blood. Dinner that day was commendably fresh.

INGREDIENTS

- 2 fresh uromastyx lizards
- ½ cup of soy sauce
- 3 tablespoons of brown sugar
- 2 garlic cloves, crushed
- 1 tablespoon of black pepper
- 1 cup of water
- Peanut or grape seed oil

METHOD

Skin and gut each lizard with a sharp knife, taking care not to cut the stomach for fear of releasing a stench of rotting vegetation that you will remember for all the wrong reasons. Remove the head and hands and throw them away. Make a marinade using the soy sauce, brown sugar, crushed garlic, black pepper and water and soak the lizards in it. Keep overnight in a refrigerator. Remove the marinated lizards, pat them dry and allow them to reach room temperature. Heat a barbecue to a high temperature, rub peanut or grape seed oil to the exteriors of the lizards and cook for about 7 minutes each side, rotating to get nice grill marks on the meat. Remove from the flame and cover in foil for 8 minutes. Serve with rice or potatoes.

Recipe: *soosmarkhor.weebly.com*

Seal flipper pie

EASTERN CANADA

At Easter, many children (and adults) across the world look forward to receiving a chocolate egg, but in Newfoundland a different kind of treat is on the Easter menu – seal flipper pie. And before you jump to the conclusion that the name is not a literal description, like the old boiled sweets known as 'bull's eyes', be assured that this is a pie containing the real flippers of real seals.

The history of the dish dates back to the early eighteenth century when seal meat was a staple food for Inuit living on the northern shores of Labrador and Newfoundland. High in vitamin A, it was the most reliable foodstuff for combating scurvy. The resourceful hunters put every part of the seal to good use (the fat was used to light lamps), but they were at a loss to think what to do with the flippers. So they invented their own special recipe – seal flipper pie. Sometimes it is just referred to as 'flipper pie', which could lead adventurous diners to expect a meal of celebrity dolphin.

As the seal flippers are very fatty, you are strongly advised to remove all the fat beforehand. Otherwise you will end up with a horrible, greasy pie which, in the words, of one who has tasted it, 'smells a lot like seal crap'. Prepared properly, the dish is considerably better than it sounds, with its rich, dark, gamey seal meat. No wonder polar bears love them so much.

So if you ever happen to find yourself in eastern Canada around Easter, take the plunge and join the seal club, although you might be advised to avoid using that particular phrase.

INGREDIENTS

- 1 tablespoon of baking soda
- 4 seal flippers
- 2 tablespoons of cooking oil
- Salt and pepper
- 1 large onion, chopped
- 2 garlic cloves, crushed
- 2 tablespoons of flour
- 2 cups of beef stock
- 1 celery stick
- 2 large carrots
- 1 turnip
- 1 parsnip
- 4 potatoes
- Pastry

METHOD

Mix the baking soda in cold water and allow the seal flippers to soak for half an hour. The baking soda solution makes all the fat on the flipper turn white, so, using this information, take a sharp knife and remove all traces of fat. Rinse the fat-free flippers and dry. Sauté both sides of the seal on medium heat in a pot in cooking oil or pork fat until lightly brown. Season the flippers, remove them from the heat and put to one side. Lower the heat to medium, add the onion and garlic and cook for about 5 minutes until the onion turns golden brown. Add the flour and continue cooking over high heat for approximately 5 minutes until the mixture is brown and bubbling. Stir in the beef stock and bring to a boil. Keep stirring until the liquid thickens. Return the flippers to the pot and cover. Simmer for 45 minutes or until the flippers are partly tender. Add the chopped celery, carrots, turnip and parsnip and simmer for 20 minutes. Add the potatoes and cook for another 20 minutes until all the vegetables are tender. Transfer the mixture to a deep casserole dish and top with pastry. Bake at 425°F (220°C) for 20–30 minutes or until the pie crust is golden brown. Serves six to eight people.

Recipe: *saltjunk.com*

Boiled polar bear with fermented walrus flipper

ALASKA

Some foods are just meant to go together – strawberries and cream, sausages and mash, fish and chips. It is the same with polar bear and walrus flipper. Apparently they complement each other perfectly; the walrus sweetens the bear meat while the bear takes away the greasy taste of the fermented flipper. So if you thought seal flipper pie was politically incorrect, try serving this traditional Alaskan Thanksgiving recipe at a Greenpeace banquet.

If you don't fancy an endangered species as your main course, you could just opt for the walrus, or *igunak* as it is known to Inuit people. After being killed, the walrus carcass is hacked into steaks with an axe and buried in ice for a year so that it ferments. Timing is everything – dig it out from the ice too early and the taste will leave a lot to be desired even by walrus standards but dig it out too late and it will have decomposed into a toxic jelly. Once dug up, it should be eaten straight away – raw. Since a single walrus can feed more than an average family, friends and neighbours are invited round to join the feast. British food writer Stefan Gates said it smelled of 'wet dog' (a trait it evidently shares with cow's womb) and tasted 'pretty much how you'd expect a twelve-month-old decomposing walrus to taste'.

Walrus can also be cooked, either in a stew with rice and onions, or the severed flipper can be put in a soup. Just don't expect it to be able to swim across the bowl.

If you ever need to ask your local butcher for a cut of polar bear, tell him you want the shoulder blade because that is considered the choicest cut. It's always handy to know these things.

INGREDIENTS
- 1 walrus flipper
- 1 polar bear
- Beef bouillon
- 2 onions
- Salt to taste

METHOD

Catch a walrus, chop it into pieces and store these tightly together in ice for a year in a bag made of walrus skin. Hack off the flipper (the rest of the meat can be used in a stew). Catch a polar bear. Dice the bear meat, making sure to leave fat on some of the chunks. Polar bear fat is drier than walrus or seal blubber, has a subtle taste and helps to keep the meat tender. Put the pieces of bear meat and slices of walrus flipper in a pot, season with bouillon, onion and salt, and boil. Serve with mixed greens.

Recipe: *alaskadispatch.com*

Haggis
SCOTLAND

You can understand why some people might have a problem with haggis. You take a sheep's offal – basically the nasty bits that nobody wants – mix it with suet and oatmeal and boil it in a bag made from the animal's stomach. Small wonder that the *Larousse Gastronomique* concedes that 'its description is not immediately appealing'.

The Scots excuse the ingredients by saying that the dish is a traditional way of using up parts of the animal that would otherwise go to waste. Some may argue that there is a very good reason for letting them go to waste. It would seem that a number of Americans are so baffled by the concept that they cannot believe haggis is even a dish. A recent online survey found that one-third of American tourists visiting Scotland thought that a haggis was a wild animal and almost a quarter arrived in Scotland thinking they could catch one. Others confused it with the bagpipes, which is fair enough because you can get a better tune out of a haggis.

The origins of what has become Scotland's national dish remain shrouded in mystery. Some historians say it dates back to the days of the Scottish cattle drovers while others claim the first haggis arrived in Scotland via a Viking longboat. The first known recipe for 'hagese' appeared around 1430 in a cookery book written in – shock, horror – England.

The modern haggis is often packed in an artificial casing instead of the traditional sheep's stomach, and some commercial haggis is made from pig, rather than sheep, offal. You can buy tinned haggis, vegetarian haggis and even haggis pizza. Haggis has gone mainstream.

There is also an international haggis hurling contest, perhaps proof that a lot of people think the best thing to do with a haggis is to throw it as far away as possible.

INGREDIENTS

- 1 sheep's stomach (empty)
- 1 sheep's pluck (heart, lungs and liver)
- 1lb of toasted oatmeal
- 1 tablespoon of salt
- 1 tablespoon of freshly ground black pepper
- 1 tablespoon of freshly ground allspice
- 1 tablespoon of mixed herbs
- 8oz of finely chopped suet
- 4 large onions

METHOD

Wash the sheep's stomach in cold water until it is thoroughly clean and then soak it in cold salted water for between 8 and 10 hours. Place the heart, liver and lungs in a large pot and cover with cold water. The sheep's windpipe ought to be hung over the side of the pot with a container beneath it in order to collect any drips. Gently simmer the pluck for approximately 2 hours or until it is tender and then leave to cool. Finely chop or mince the pluck and then mix it with the oatmeal. Add about half a pint of the stock in which the meat was cooked and add the seasonings, suet and finely chopped onion. Mix together well. Fill the stomach with the mixture, leaving enough room for the oatmeal to expand. Press out the air and then sew up the haggis. Prick the haggis a few times with a fine needle. Place the haggis in boiling water and simmer for approximately 3 hours.

Recipe: *The Glasgow Cookery Book*, 1926

Rancid bear paw

ANCIENT CHINA

Bear paw was a favourite dish of King Zhou, who was the last monarch of ancient China's Shang dynasty and had something of a reputation as a torturer, drinker and host of extravagant orgies. According to legend, after his death in 1046BC, the gods decided to deify him but, finding nothing suitable, they created a post specially for him: God of Sodomy. This tells you all you need to know about King Zhou.

He was also reputedly strong enough to hunt and kill wild beasts with his bare hands. Whether or not this extended to bear is uncertain, but the animal's meat was considered a delicacy at his outrageous banquets as the course between the mass orgy and the one where prisoners suffered a slow, painful death by being forced to hug a large bronze cylinder filled with red-hot charcoal. So prized was bear's paw that the Chinese philosopher Mencius once said: 'If I cannot have both bear's paws and fish, then I would prefer bear's paws.'

Thankfully bear is rarely found in today's Chinese restaurants, but there is still a black market trade in the paws. In 2013, Chinese authorities seized 213 bear paws, worth a total of nearly $500,000, from a truck crossing from Russia to Inner Mongolia. They were destined to be eaten, used for medicinal purposes or just as exotic gifts.

The ancient recipe below for bear's paw recommends leaving it to go rancid for up to two years before cooking. Modern methods for stewing or roasting bear's paw are much quicker. After removing as much fur from the paw as possible, you plaster it with mud and bake in an oven. This should clear away any remaining fur, after which the paw is placed in boiling water and then soaked in more water for a couple of days. The paw should now be soft, allowing you to skin it and remove the bones, leaving you with just the meat, which can then be cooked as required.

So is bear's paw worth all the effort? Chinese gourmet Xi Feng certainly thinks so, describing the taste as 'sweet and fat, even better than shark's fin'. That is clearly intended to be a compliment. He added: 'It is like pork cooked at the right time and temperature, but smooth and soft, and not as greasy as pork fat'.

Those who are fussy about their bear's paws prefer – and will therefore pay more for – the left front paw, because when the bear is hibernating, it licks that particular paw. This means that its salivary secretions are concentrated on the left front paw, making it the most nutritious. By contrast, the back paws are tougher and therefore less desirable from having been walked on. Nevertheless they are of great value to the bear, but sadly King Zhou's general mindset meant that this would not have warranted consideration.

INGREDIENTS

- 1 bear paw
- Lime
- Fried rice
- 2oz of honey
- 1 teaspoon of salt
- 20oz of chicken broth
- 1/3 oz of ginger
- 7oz grain alcohol

METHOD

The bear paw cannot be eaten immediately after it is cut off. It is necessary to let it go rancid for one or two years before cooking. Clean the paw with paper. Don't use water that might contaminate it. Put some lime in a bowl, then add a thick layer of fried rice. Place the bear paw on the rice and cover it with another layer of rice. Put a lid on the bowl and seal it with lime. Once the paw has finally gone rancid, peel it and clean it before coating it in a thick layer of honey. Cook in a pot at low heat for 1 hour. Rinse the paw, then simmer for 3 hours in a pot with the chicken broth and seasonings on the embers of a fire.

Recipe: *www.nytimes.com*

Deep-fried frog burger

JAPAN

If finding a black burger bun on the menu wasn't odd enough, Japan's Orbi Yokohama Museum Café took to filling it with a very large, whole deep-fried frog. While a standard beefburger bears no physical resemblance to a cow, the same could not be said of the frog burger, which gave the distinct impression of containing an amphibian that had just been flattened by a steam roller. It's not a good look for a frog and it's not a good look for a burger either, especially as there is something deeply unsettling about eating a burger where the legs of the occupant protrude several inches from one side of the bun.

Equally worryingly, the limited edition frog burger was created in 2015 to celebrate the museum's Deadly Poison Exhibition (some species of frog are highly venomous), an unconventionally themed menu if ever there was one. However, the proprietor was quick to point out that the frogs used in the recipe were harmless. To make up for it, round, seedless, bamboo-charcoal buns were used to add a sinister note, although the smooth black bun perched on top of the frog looked more like an old-style crash helmet. Indeed the overall effect of the presentation suggested that the Crazy Frog had suffered a nasty accident, which in itself was no bad thing.

INGREDIENTS
- 1 frog
- 1 burger bun
- Lettuce
- Chilli sauce

METHOD

Deep fry the frog and insert it between the two halves of the burger bun. Garnish with lettuce and chilli sauce. Try and pretend that you are eating chicken.

Recipe: *en.rocketnews24.com*

Tadpole casserole

THAILAND

With frog playing such a prominent role in various national cuisines, it is inevitable that someone would find a culinary use for tadpoles, too. Enter *mok huak*, a Thai dish in which dozens of tadpoles are mixed with chillies and herbs before being wrapped and cooked in a parcel of banana leaves.

For a fuller flavour, it is suggested that the tadpoles are selected at the stage when they have just started to grow legs and that they are kept in clean water overnight before cooking. However if they are still a little on the bland side, you could either deep fry them for a taste said to be the equal of chicken nuggets (as if that's a good thing) or add some fermented fish sauce to provide the sort of kick that the hapless tadpole can no longer muster.

CNN travel writer Mark Wiens was not impressed, writing: 'If a plate full of developing frog tadpoles doesn't already make you want to puke, add a generous dose of fermented fish sauce (*pla raa*) to the equation and you might just have the most repulsive dish available in the world of Thai cuisine'.

The advantage of tadpole over frog is the lack of bones, but if you feel squeamish about cutting short a life at such an early stage, remember that the tadpole survival rate in the wild is miniscule, so by popping them in a wok you're simply speeding up nature.

When all is said and done, being wrapped in a lovely banana leaf and enjoying a nice sauna is probably preferable to being slowly tortured by a psychotic cat or speared by a heron's beak.

INGREDIENTS

- Lemongrass
- Chillies
- Sweet basil
- Dill
- 1 handful of tadpoles
- Banana leaves

METHOD

Mix the lemongrass, chillies, sweet basil and dill in a bowl and add a handful of fresh tadpoles. Spoon the tadpole mixture into a few layers of banana leaves, and fold the leaves together, tying them in place like a parcel. Place the parcel on a low grill for about 10 minutes until it has finished cooking.

Recipe: *migrationology.com*

Seal brain fritters

INUIT

___

If you are not averse to a recipe which contains the instruction 'mash the brains', then seal brain fritters may be for you. Gerald Cutland, a chef on a British Antarctic expedition in the 1950s, devised various recipes for seal brains, which he called 'one of the delicacies of the Antarctic'. They included fried seal brains, seal brains *au gratin*, seal brain omelette, savoury seal brains on toast and seal brain fritters, which he described as 'an excellent breakfast dish', which was 'enjoyed by most members of the base when I was chef'. It was certainly an interesting way to start the day.

Cutland was also very fond of a shag, but purely in a culinary sense. Extolling the virtues of cooking the sea bird, he said that if you haven't tried one you're 'missing one of the luxuries of the Antarctic'. To underline his point, he advised: 'If you see any around, take a .22 rifle and knock a few off. It is a very meaty bird and one is enough for about six people.'

No matter how popular they were with Cutland's colleagues, seal brains are now largely off the menu with Antarctic explorers, but they are still eaten at the other end of the world by Inuit. Some recipes are simply too good not to be shared.

- 2 seal brains
- 1 tablespoon of salt
- 1 tablespoon of vinegar
- ½ cup of flour
- 2 tablespoons of egg powder
- ¼ cup of milk
- 2 tablespoons of melted butter
- ¼ teaspoon of mixed herbs
- ½ teaspoon of salt
- ¼ teaspoon of pepper
- Fat for deep frying

METHOD

Wash the seal brains in salted water. Remove the loose skin and
blood. Soak the brains in fresh cold water for an hour, changing the
water two or three times. Cover with water to which a tablespoon
of salt and a tablespoon of vinegar have been added and boil for
15 minutes. Drain and pat dry. Mash the brains until soft and light.
Mix the flour, egg powder and milk together, beating well to make
a soft, smooth batter. Add the brains, melted butter, herbs, salt
and pepper to the batter and mix well. Drop tablespoons of the
mixture into hot fat and deep fry until golden brown. Drain the
fritters well. Serves four.

Recipe: *Northern Cookbook*, edited by Eleanor A. Ellis, 1967

Baked armadillo

Should you be considering putting armadillo on your dinner menu, there are four factors in its favour. It has poor eyesight and poor hearing (both of which make it relatively easy to catch), it is not legally protected and the chances of catching leprosy from eating one are pretty slim. Armadillos are the only animals apart from humans that carry leprosy and have been linked to cases of the disease in humans in the Deep South, so as a precaution you should never undercook them. If you go to a restaurant where they serve armadillo tartare, run a mile. An armadillo actually produces a lot of meat, although the smaller ones are usually the best for frying. The older ones need to be cooked slowly for a long time to ensure that their meat is tender, because what could be worse for a redneck society hostess to hear than 'this armadillo's a bit chewy, woman'?

Another good reason for eating them is that there are an estimated 50 million armadillos in the United States, compared to, for example, just 50,000 nuns. So it makes sound ecological sense to bait, trap and bake armadillos in preference to nuns.

A century ago, armadillos provided meat for many a pioneer household, earning the nickname 'possum on the half-shell'. Later during the Great Depression they were called 'Hoover hogs', an ironic acknowledgement of Herbert Hoover's 1928 election promise of 'a chicken in every pot' when in reality many people were so poor that they could only eat what they could catch – and that was often armadillo, so long as you stood downwind because one sense that armadillos do possess is a keen recognition of smell.

The meat is said to taste a bit like pork, but is also used as a substitute for chicken and beef in various dishes. As well as baked armadillo, recipes can be found for, among others, fried armadillo, armadillo in mustard sauce, smoked armadillo chops, armadillo chilli, armadillo *fricassée* and armadillo meatloaf. In some South American countries, they grill armadillo in the shell (after gutting it), split side down. It is then eaten out of the shell, conveniently saving the need for pans and plates. The idea of eating armadillo may not necessarily appeal to everybody, but the next time you are planning a romantic meal, why not surprise your loved one? Just try not to think about the leprosy.

INGREDIENTS
- 1 armadillo
- Salt
- Pepper
- 1½ cups of apple
- 1½ cups of pineapple
- ½ cup of butter

METHOD

Cut the armadillo from its shell and wash the meat thoroughly.
Add salt and pepper and stuff it with apple and pineapple. Coat
with butter, wrap in foil and place in a roasting pan. Bake at 350°F
(180°C), allowing 30–45 minutes per pound. Allow only about 5oz
of armadillo meat per serving. You can have too much of a good
thing.

Recipe: *www.cooks.com*

Whole stuffed camel

SAUDI ARABIA

Guinness World Records acknowledge whole roasted camel – a dish prepared occasionally for Bedouin wedding feasts – as the largest item on any menu in the world. The book adds that 'cooked eggs are stuffed into fish, the fish stuffed into cooked chickens, the chickens stuffed into a roasted sheep's carcass and the sheep stuffed into a whole camel'. So if you thought your family's Christmas turkey was big, think again. Even Adam Richman on *Man v. Food* would draw the line at attacking a whole camel.

Camel meat has been on Middle Eastern menus for centuries, and a whole roasted camel was recorded as a dish at a banquet in ancient Persia. An entire camel is way too much meat for the average family, so the dish is reserved primarily for large gatherings, especially weddings. So it won't only be the bride's mother who gets the hump.

The nearest thing to a complete recipe for this extravaganza was allegedly compiled by a group of Californian home economics teachers in the 1980s, although it omits the fish, possibly fearing a clash of flavours with the lamb, chicken and camel. Then again, surf and turf was all the rage back then. Of greater concern in the recipe (overleaf) is how anyone would be able to obtain a cooking pot large enough to accommodate and boil an entire camel. You would need a Jacuzzi, and who would want to climb into a hot tub for a relaxing dip knowing that the previous occupant was a dead camel? A more practical method, therefore, might be to forget about pre-boiling the camel but instead to stuff it with the cooked chickens and lamb and then just roast it over the charcoal pit. However, this raises the problem that the camel meat might not be as tender as desired and could be excessively fatty. Or you could just hack the raw camel into sections (neck, rump, belly and legs) before boiling and stuffing with the other meats, but obviously this would not look as aesthetically pleasing when served on a giant platter.

These major considerations were mere trifles to Chinese celebrity chef Momin Hopur, who, in 2015, succeeded in roasting a whole 990lb camel for the annual Apricot Tourism Festival in Xinjiang. Using more than 10,000 bricks, he and his team of apprentices spent five days building a six-metre-high kiln, which was then pre-heated for 48 hours. They lowered the camel, which had been coated in a yellow marinade of eggs, black pepper and 36 herbs, into the kiln by crane and allowed it to cook for five hours. Hundreds queued for three hours to grab a piece of camel.

In 2007, French chef Christian Falco, who specialized in roasting massive cuts of meat, had tackled an even bigger beast, spit-roasting a 1,200lb camel for fifteen hours over three tons of wood in the Moroccan seaside town of Safi. The feast fed 500 guests. 'It's a tradition that's fallen out of favour,' lamented Falco afterwards, recalling an occasion two centuries earlier when the King of Morocco had offered a roasted camel to his subjects.

Camel meat is generally low in cholesterol, but high in iron and protein. Its taste has been compared to beef or venison. In Syria, the fatty hump is considered to be the best part and such a delicacy that some people choose to eat it raw.

INGREDIENTS

- 1 medium-sized camel
- 1 large lamb
- 20 chickens
- 110 gallons of water
- 12kg of rice
- 2kg of pine nuts
- 2kg of almonds
- 1kg of pistachio nuts
- 5lb black pepper
- Salt to taste
- 60 eggs

METHOD

Skin, trim and clean the camel, the lamb and the chickens and boil all 22 creatures until they are tender. This may take a little longer for the camel than the chickens. Cook the rice until it is fluffy. Fry the nuts until brown and mix with the rice, black pepper and salt to taste. Hard boil the eggs and peel. Stuff the cooked chickens with the hard-boiled eggs and rice. Stuff the cooked lamb with the stuffed chickens. Add more rice. Stuff the camel with the stuffed lamb and add the rest of the rice. Broil the camel over a large charcoal pit until it is brown. Spread on a large tray and decorate with boiled eggs and nuts. The whole cooking process takes about 24 hours. Serves between 80 and 100 people.

Recipe: *www.food.com*

Live octopus

KOREA

As a general rule of thumb, it is advisable to ensure that any creature on your dinner plate is dead before you eat it, particularly if it is capable of exacting revenge on the way down. Yet Korean cuisine champions *sannakji*, a live baby octopus, which, even though it has been chopped into small pieces, is so fresh when served that the suction cups on its tentacles are still active and can cling to your tongue and throat as you try to swallow it, making you choke uncontrollably. This is a meal that does not give up without a fight.

A number of cases have been reported of diners choking to death on partially-chewed segments of live octopus, especially when inebriated. For this reason, customers are urged to chew each piece thoroughly and to douse the dish in sesame oil, which makes it more difficult for the writhing octopus to form a serious grip on your throat. On the other hand, the tentacles are said to react angrily when drenched in hot, spicy sauce.

At Korean fish markets, live octopi are widely offered for sale in water-filled bags to keep them in good shape for the chopping board. The introduction of a sharp knife to its body does nothing to quell the octopus's movement due to residual nerve activity that can keep its tentacles wriggling for up to thirty minutes following dissection. At this point the first-time diner will also have nerves that are shredded. Despite the potential dangers of the dish, seasoned *sannakji* eaters actually enjoy the sensation of the squirming tentacles sliding down their throat.

Some brave souls don't even bother chopping up the octopus. Instead they eat it whole, including the head. To demonstrate their courage and to build up their strength, Kendo martial arts

fighters traditionally eat an entire baby octopus wrapped around chopsticks. However, only the largest mouths can accommodate such a feast and if you think dealing with one tentacle is tough, try chewing eight thrashing limbs simultaneously, each one trying furiously to grab your lips and cheeks. Besides, how disconcerting must it be to have a live octopus looking you right in the eye at close quarters while you eat its arms?

INGREDIENTS
- 1 small octopus
- Sesame seeds
- 1 cup of sesame oil

METHOD
Chop the live octopus into small pieces, season with sesame seeds and serve immediately. Dip each tentacle in sesame oil before eating and chew thoroughly.

Recipe: *Daily Mail*

Soured herring

SWEDEN

Surströmming is a fermented Baltic Sea herring possessing such a foul smell that when a can of it smashes to the floor in a Swedish supermarket, they generally evacuate the store. It is almost always eaten outside – in fact, it is illegal to take _surströmming_ into apartment buildings in Stockholm. In 1981, a German landlord evicted a tenant without notice for spreading _surströmming_ brine in the staircase of the apartment building. The landlord was taken to court, where he successfully proved his case by opening a can of _surströmming_ in the courtroom. The court concluded that it 'had convinced itself that the disgusting smell of the fish brine far exceeded the degree that fellow tenants in the building could be expected to tolerate.' In 2014, a Japanese study declared a newly opened can of _surströmming_ to be the worst smelling food on the planet. The Swedes considered it an accolade.

Cans of _surströmming_ have also been known to explode, prompting British Airways and Air France to ban it from flights. Acting in sympathy, Stockholm's international airport withdrew it from sale. In 2014, a fire at a Swedish warehouse containing 1,000 cans of _surströmming_ caused explosions that lasted for six hours, launching cans all over the surrounding area.

It has been a staple of northern Swedish cuisine for over 500 years. Back in the sixteenth century, it was supplied as army rations to Swedish troops fighting the Thirty Years War. Foreign conscripts and those Swedish soldiers who were unfamiliar with *surströmming* flatly refused to eat it, but at least its very presence probably helped keep the enemy at bay. There is even a Surströmming Museum, located way up in the north of the country in about as isolated a spot as could be found. It opened its doors (but only slightly) in 2005. *Surströmming* is widely sold in cans but should you be misguided enough to wish to make your own, you are recommended to buy your herring in May or June, which will leave plenty of time for them to ferment before the traditional *surströmming* feasting time of late August. If you buy them any earlier, the fermented mixture will be hanging around the house for longer than your family will be able to stomach.

You will need a long stick, firstly for stirring the fermenting herring, and secondly to shoo the neighbourhood cats away. You will also need three buckets – one for the reserved brine, a second for temporarily holding the fish while draining off the first brining, and a third to be sick in. Indeed German food critic Wolfgang Fassbender proclaimed that 'the biggest challenge when eating *surströmming* is to vomit only after the first bite, as opposed to before'.

- About 80lb of freshly caught herring
- 1 large barrel with ventilation valve
- Salt water for brining

METHOD

Brine the herring for a day in a salt concentration that measures around 23 degrees on a salinometer. Decapitate, clean and gut the herring and pack into a large barrel, leaving an inch for any gas to escape without causing an explosion. Leave the barrel out in the sun for 24 hours to start the fermentation process, stirring every 3 hours to achieve an even putrefaction. Reserve about 5 quarts of brine and pour off the rest. Mix the reserved brine back in and add five gallons of 12-degree brine. Move the barrel indoors to a dark place at a temperature of 63°– 65°F and allow the fermentation to continue for at least 2 months. It is traditionally served with new potatoes and onion on thin slices of bread, and because of its high salt content, is always accompanied by large quantities of liquid refreshment. The Visit Sweden website advises it to be served with 'beer, schnapps and lots of friends'. Bear in mind, however, that if you serve them *surströmming*, they might not be friends for long.

Recipe: *www.ehow.com*

Pufferfish

JAPAN

There are so many species of fish in the world's rivers and oceans that you have to question why anyone would want to eat one that is so toxic it can kill you if it is not prepared properly. *Fugu* (or pufferfish, blowfish or balloonfish as it is also known) contains lethal amounts of the poison tetrodotoxin in its organs, especially the liver, ovaries and eyes. This poison, for which there is no known antidote, is around 1,250 times more powerful than cyanide and leads to a particularly unpleasant death. It paralyzes the muscles, leaving the victim unable to breathe while remaining fully conscious until he or she eventually dies from asphyxiation. Death from *fugu* has been compared to death from a nerve agent like Sarin. On the plus side, it's tasty with chips.

Just one milligram of its toxin could be fatal, but a typical mature *fugu* contains thirty times that amount. Ironically by fish standards, it has quite an appealing face, and with its big eyes and inflated body, it could easily have been designed by Disney. Certainly if you had to choose between a cod and a pufferfish on a marine date, you would go for the latter. In this instance, looks can be deceptive.

Due to the high probability that a badly-prepared dish of *fugu* might be your last supper, Japanese law states that only restaurant chefs who have qualified after two years of stringent training are permitted to prepare the fish for consumption. Their course includes an all-important identification test as some types of pufferfish (notably the tiger blowfish) are more poisonous than others. To prevent contamination, the knives used to slice the fish are stored separately from the rest of the kitchen utensils, but even so the chefs know that when cutting the fish apart they are literally dicing with death. The fish is gutted, but so will you be if it is not done correctly.

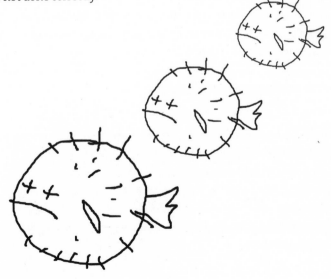

Fugu has been eaten in Japan and China for centuries, although it has also been banned periodically. According to folklore, fishermen claimed that its poison could be reversed by burying victims up to their head in sand. As yet, there is no firm scientific proof that this treatment is effective. It is the only food that the Emperor of Japan is forbidden to eat, purely for his own safety. It is sod's law that what is said to be the tastiest part, the liver, is also the most toxic, as a result of which serving the liver in Japanese restaurants was banned outright in 1984. As chefs became wise to the dangers of certain body parts, most fatalities occurred following a meal of *fugu* cooked at home, often by anglers eager to sample their catch. Never has the warning 'Don't try this at home' been more appropriate. In any case it is now illegal to sell a whole fish to the public. They just can't be trusted.

The highest profile casualty was actor and 'national treasure' Bando Mitsugoro VIII who died in 1975 a few hours after eating four helpings of *fugu* liver. He claimed to be able to resist the poison, but his confidence proved somewhat misplaced. More recently, fifteen people in Thailand were killed and 115 were hospitalized over a three-year period after unscrupulous fish sellers dyed the banned pufferfish pink and sold them disguised as salmon.

Because of its notoriety, *fugu* has become an exclusive and expensive dish – fried, grilled, baked or stewed. It is sometimes served in wafer-thin slices arranged on the plate in the shape of a flying crane, a symbol of longevity. This is tantamount to a prayer. Pufferfish skin is not usually poisonous, so once any spikes have been pulled out, the skin can be eaten as part of a salad called *yubiki*.

Incredibly some daredevils still view eating the banned but deadly liver as a challenge, deriving a particular thrill from the tingling sensation that the neurotoxin in the fish's organs leaves on their lips. In 2015, five Japanese men were rushed to hospital after experiencing breathing difficulties and vomiting, having expressly requested that a restaurant in Wakayama serve them the liver. The restaurant was subsequently shut down by city officials, but the incident will do little to dissuade others from playing what has been likened to the culinary version of Russian roulette.

METHOD
Leave it to the professionals.

DESSERTS

Blood ice cream

UNITED STATES

Coming from a nation where black pudding is considered a delicacy in some quarters, we should not really throw up our hands in horror at the thought of eating blood. But blood ice cream? Ice cream should conjure up images of summer fruits and berries not the insides of an animal. Yet manufacturers from Denmark to Canada are sanguine that blood ice cream will catch on, with pork blood replacing egg whites in the creative process. They point out that blood is rich in iron and protein and a complete food when mixed with milk. They do so while carefully avoiding any mention of the V-word, because even the world's best sales pitch might cut no ice when the vampire factor is taken into consideration. It is hard to imagine someone who considers any flavour other than vanilla to be racy suddenly taking to pork blood ice cream.

Blood ice cream looks pretty much like a delicious dark chocolate but has the decidedly livery taste that you might expect, although in the recipe below that effect is lessened by the presence of the orange zest. A Washington, DC restaurant, The Pig – dedicated to all things porky – went a step further by devising a pork blood ice cream sundae, named, appropriately enough, Sundae Bloody Sundae. Chef Garret Fleming explained that the local butcher he usually deals with was not legally allowed to sell him pig's blood, so he had to source it from Asian markets. When his sous chef went to collect it, he received some curious looks for saying, 'I'd like ten gallons of your pig's blood'.

Those looks, however, would be mild compared to the one you would receive from Aunt Mildred should you inform her that the nice chocolate ice cream she thought she had just licked from the cone was, in fact, pork blood.

INGREDIENTS

- ³/₄ cup of sugar
- ¹/₃ cup of alkalized cocoa
- 2 tablespoons of cornstarch
- ¹/₂ teaspoon of ground ginger
- 1 pinch of fine sea salt
- 1 cup of milk
- ¹/₂ cup of pork blood
- Finely grated zest of an orange

Place the sugar in a bowl, then sift in the cocoa and cornstarch. Add the ginger and salt and gradually whisk in the milk until the mixture is smooth. Pour in the blood and whisk to combine. Pour the mixture into a saucepan and place over medium heat until it boils, stirring constantly to make sure it doesn't stick to the side of the pan. Remove the pan from the heat and stir in the orange zest. Transfer the mixture, which should now be thick and dark, into a bowl and place a piece of cling film on the surface to prevent skin forming. Allow to cool and then refrigerate until it sets.

Recipe: *www.foxnews.com*

Eskimo ice cream

ALASKA

If an Inuit offers you an ice cream, you might be advised to think twice before accepting too eagerly. For although Eskimo ice cream (or *akutaq*) looks the part, it is unlike any ice cream we know, being made from a combination of reindeer fat, seal oil, fresh snow, berries and, sometimes as an added treat, ground fish. And they don't even stick a chocolate flake in the top.

Akutaq has been made by the indigenous people of Alaska for centuries, often taken on hunting expeditions as a survival food but also used for domestic ceremonies like funerals or parties. If reindeer or seal were in short supply, they would substitute moose or walrus, as you do. The type of animal fat used determines the taste of the ice cream. Well-aged yellow fat is considered preferable because it has more flavour and whips up into a lighter, fluffier texture than fresh fat. With sugar hard to come by in the Arctic regions, berries are relied on to provide the sweetness. Apparently when an Inuit woman comes to choose which berries to put in her ice cream it is a once-in-a- lifetime decision, with any attempt to switch to another kind of berry bringing about a loss of social status. However, it is acceptable to eat ice cream made from a different type of berry from your own. Cranberries, blueberries, salmonberries, crowberries and cloudberries are the most common.

Inuit love to offer outsiders a taste of *akutaq*, if only to see the look on their faces when they realize that their dessert owes more to reindeer fat and seal oil than cow's milk. *What's Cooking America* has advice on how to behave in such circumstances. 'If you are a guest and are offered some (you will probably be served first as a guest), at least try a small amount. Please do not express any "yucks" or other words of ridicule. If you really cannot bring yourself to eat this unusual food, accept the serving and find the oldest person in the room and offer the food to him or her. This will show that you have good manners, if not good taste, and that you respect your elders.'

This is useful to know as it seems that Inuit etiquette can be a bit of a minefield.

As for the taste, let's just say that there is an ice cream parlour in Merida, Venezuela, which sells almost 900 different flavours – and *akutaq* isn't one of them.

INGREDIENTS

- 1 cup of reindeer fat
- 1 cup of seal oil
- 2 cups of fresh, loose snow
- 3 cups of fresh berries

METHOD

Grind the reindeer fat into small pieces. Place it in a pot over low heat and stir until it becomes a liquid. Add one-third of the cup of seal oil, and mix it in. Remove the pan from the heat and continue stirring. Add one cup of snow and another third of the seal oil. As the fat cools and begins to turn fluffy and white, add the remaining snow and seal oil, stirring all the time. When the mixture is as fluffy and white as you can make it, fold in the berries. Freeze so that it firms up and is ready to eat.

Recipe: *whatscookingamerica.net*

Frog fallopian tubes

CHINA

The bad news about the Chinese dessert ingredient *hasma* **(or** *hashima***) is that it is made from the fatty tissue found near the fallopian tubes of female snow frogs.** The good news is that it is available – albeit not cheaply – in packs in Chinese supermarkets or herbal stores, so there is no need to get up close and personal with a frog.

The frog hunters of the mountainous north-east of the country have done that for you. The white-bellied female frogs are killed, strung together through their mouths and hung up to dry for later use, like a line of underwear with legs. Sometimes also known as snow jelly, *hasma* is usually sold dried in irregular flat pieces, but when rehydrated these pieces can expand up to twenty times in size and acquire a translucent, slithery, gelatinous appearance, not unlike snot. It has a slightly fishy smell and is often served in sweet dessert soups with red dates, longan fruits or lotus seeds. When cooked, its light, chewy texture has also been compared to tapioca, which, coincidentally, was regularly called frogspawn by British children when it was a staple of school dinners in the 1950s.

Hasma is regarded as a health food, supposedly offering increased strength and energy, especially after childbirth, and a clearer complexion. So if you don't fancy eating the stuff, you can always rub it on your face. That's a choice you don't get with crème brulée.

INGREDIENTS

- ½ tablespoon of *hasma* (fallopian tubes)
- 4 cups of water
- 1 fresh medium ginger, finely sliced
- 12 almonds, skinned
- 4 pitted dried red dates
- 1 tablespoon of rock sugar

METHOD

Soak the *hasma* for 2 hours in fresh warm tap water, then drain and rinse well. If any pieces are too large, cut them to size. Bring 2 cups of cold water to the boil. Add the *hasma* with the sliced ginger and simmer for 10 minutes. Drain and put to one side, but keep the liquid. Put the *hasma*, its liquid, the dates and the skinned almonds into a bowl. Add 2 more cups of water and cover tightly. Place in a steamer and steam over boiling water for 2 hours. before adding the sugar and steaming for another half hour. Serve warm.

Recipe: *www.flavorandfortune.com*

Durian
INDONESIA

___

Known as the 'King of Fruits' in south-east Asia, the durian has a colourful fragrance which has been variously described as reminiscent of old gym socks, dead rats, turpentine, skunk spray, raw sewage, stale vomit, rotting flesh, dirty nappies or used surgical swabs – and that's even before it has been opened. Its stench is so repulsive that animals can smell it half a mile away and passengers are banned from taking it on most public transport systems, although it is unlikely that an inspector would want to get close enough to throw you off. By the same reckoning, if you ever want to be sure of getting a seat during rush-hour in Jakarta, just turn up carrying a durian.

Even if you buy a durian at a market and take it home by car, you are strongly advised to keep the windows open lest any passers-by think you are hiding a decomposing corpse on the back seat. It is also banned in many airports and hotel rooms.

One of the first westerners to describe the unusual taste of the durian was British naturalist Alfred Russel Wallace, who, in 1856, wrote: 'A rich custard highly flavoured with almonds gives the best general idea of it, but there are occasional wafts of flavour that call to mind cream cheese, onion sauce, sherry wine and other incongruous dishes'. More recently, American chef Anthony

Bourdain said that eating a durian will make your breath 'smell as if you'd been French-kissing your dead grandmother'. It is unclear how he was able to arrive at that comparison.

Those new to the durian experience should try and select a relatively young fruit as both the taste and smell will be milder. The fruit is ripe when the large, oval-shaped thorny exterior, which gives it the look of a particularly sadistic medieval weapon, begins to crack open unaided. Some daredevils like to let it ripen even beyond that stage until the flesh is creamy, slightly alcoholic and alarmingly pungent. These are usually people who have lost – or at least temporarily mislaid – their senses of taste and smell.

The fruit grows high on trees and durian farmers often wear helmets to avoid injury from the falling five-pound spike-bombs. Opening a durian is an unpleasant, messy task. You can ask the vendor to do it for you, provided he keeps a gas mask handy. Even so, make sure you have an airtight container in which to store it on your way home. It is more environmentally friendly to open it yourself at home, which you can do either with a sharp knife or simply by standing firmly on the fruit with thick-soled shoes. Do not attempt this while wearing only socks or the sensation will be like stepping barefoot on an upturned three-pin plug in the middle of the night.

Maggot cheese

SARDINIA

Call me old-fashioned but I like to see my cheese sitting quietly, motionless, on the plate minding its own business. I do not want to see it crawling with maggots, which, when placed on a nicely salted biscuit, might munch through their way it before I get the chance. Yet a mouthful of wriggling larvae is precisely what you will get if you order *casu marzu* from the cheese board on the Mediterranean island of Sardinia.

A sheep's milk cheese that has been made by Sardinians for hundreds of years, *casu marzu* (which ominously translates as 'rotten cheese') is created by leaving a whole pecorino cheese outdoors with part of the rind removed to allow the eggs of the cheese fly *Piophila casei* to be laid in the wheel. A female cheese fly can lay more than 500 eggs at a time and it is a sobering thought that by the time *casu marzu* is ready for consumption, it will contain thousands of these maggots. Once the eggs have hatched, the small, translucent larvae start eating their way relentlessly through the cheese, decomposing the fats through digestion and excreting the remains. So not only is the cheese infested with maggots, the actual cheesy bits are filled with their poop. Unsurprisingly this does not appeal to everyone, but in defence of the larvae their activities do give *casu marzu* an extremely soft texture – so soft that when prodded it oozes a stinky liquid known as 'tears'.

Although only around 0.3 inches long, the tiny worms can launch themselves distances of up to six inches in the air when disturbed, which is the equivalent of Russia's 2012 Olympic high jump champion Ivan Ukhov jumping 126 feet. Sardinian diners, who usually eat the cheese on a slice of crisp flatbread, hold a hand above the bread as they raise it to their mouth in order to prevent the maggots leaping into their eyeballs, at which they are said to aim unerringly. This must be the only cheese in the world for which you need to wear a pair of protective goggles. Alternatively locals make a cheese sandwich with two slices of flatbread, which they clamp firmly in place to stop the maggots escaping. The last thing you want to see is your lunch hopping off down the road.

Understandably some people prefer to remove the maggots from the cheese before eating it. Rather than using a pair of tweezers, they usually place the cheese in a sealed paper bag where the larvae, starved of oxygen, soon die. When the pitter-patter of maggot on paper bag ceases, you know that the last one has perished. But be careful what you wish for, because Sardinians claim that *casu marzu* is only safe to eat when the maggots are still alive. Perhaps 'safe' is something of an exaggeration because in 2008 it was named the world's most dangerous cheese by Guinness World Records. Its notoriety stems from the belief that the larvae can pass through the human stomach undigested, sometimes surviving long enough to breed in the intestine, the walls of which they subsequently attempt to dig through, causing nausea, vomiting and bloody diarrhoea. Others report experiencing days of crawling skin sensations after eating *casu marzu*.

Under European Union food hygiene regulations, *casu marzu* has been declared illegal with offenders facing hefty fines. However, you could still buy it on the black market, where it is often sold for double the price of a block of ordinary pecorino. Recently Sardinians have tried to skirt around the ban by saying the cheese is a traditional food, to which normal hygiene rules do not apply.

As if the presence of maggots were not enough, *casu marzu* has an aftertaste that can burn your tongue and last for several hours. It is not a cheese you will forget in a hurry.

Wasp crackers

JAPAN

Few things go better with cheese than a nice cracker. Unfortunately in Japan their idea of a nice cracker is to put half a dozen wasps in it. The kindest thing most of us can say about wasps is that they carry off that tricky black-and-yellow colour combination fairly well, but in the Japanese town of Omachi – about 100 miles from Tokyo – they have turned digger wasps into a rice cracker, the *jibachi senbei*.

The idea came about because, believe it or not, the digger wasp has its very own fan club in Japan, and these disciples decided that the best way to honour their idol was to trap it and kill it. Let us hope that the Justin Bieber Fan Club is taking note.

The wasp hunters, most of whom are of pensionable age, catch the insects in forests before boiling them in water. The dead wasps are dried and added to the cracker mix, which is then stamped in a hot iron cracker cutter. According to Rocket24 News, who tasted some, the wasps in the crackers are 'very much like raisins but had a slightly acidic and bitter taste to them'. As has been pointed out, you too would be bitter if you had just been boiled alive.

So if they taste like raisins, why not just use raisins? After all, raisins don't have wings that can get stuck in your teeth nor, to my knowledge, has anyone ever been stung by a raisin.

A bag of twenty wasp crackers costs around £1.60, but because only those caught in the wild have the necessary flavour, output is limited. That may be something to be thankful for.

Civet poo coffee

INDONESIA

It says much about our taste for the exotic that one of the world's most expensive coffees is made from berries that have been eaten and defecated by the Asian palm civet. A cup of *kopi luwak* can cost $80, which is a lot of money for what is essentially runny poo.

The jungle cat is very much the middle man in the whole process. It eats the berries from a coffee tree, but is unable to digest the beans inside, so it obligingly poops them out. A harvester then collects the defecated beans, processes them and pockets the money from their sale. Without the civet's intervention, *kopi luwak* would be just another coffee. When the berries pass through the animal's digestive system, the enzymes which occur naturally in the animal's gut break down the bitter proteins in the bean, and this sparks off a fermentation process that reduces the bitterness and acidity of the coffee, giving it a unique smooth flavour. One master roaster has described the taste as 'fermented plum and dark chocolate with hints of caramel and hazelnuts'. And not a hint of civet crap.

The price is driven up partly by its rarity but also by a sales pitch which claims that since the civet chooses to eat the berries in the first place, it must be selecting the best coffee berries available. Basically the customer is relying on the civet assuming the role of a feline version of the Man from Del Monte.

Of course, no two cups of *kopi luwak* will ever be exactly the same unless they have been passed by the same animal. Different civets have different overall diets, different states of health and different digestive systems. The only thing that is consistent about *kopi luwak* is the price.

Its origins date back to the 1700s when Dutch colonists created coffee plantations on the Dutch East Indies islands of Sumatra and Java. Enterprising local farmers discovered that the Asian palm civet ate the Arabica coffee berries and left the beans inside them undigested in its poop. In much the same way that someone first decided that an egg might be suitable to eat, they collected the beans from the poop, cleaned and roasted them and brewed their own coffee. The aroma came to the attention of the Dutch colonists and plantation owners who soon adopted it as their favourite coffee.

Kopi luwak earned an honourable mention in the 2008 movie *The Bucket List* when Carter Chambers (played by Morgan Freeman) reveals with amusement how the coffee that Edward Cole (Jack Nicholson) had so enjoyed had been produced from the poop of a jungle cat. 'You're shitting me!' exclaimed Cole in disbelief. 'No,' replied Chambers wryly, 'the cats beat me to it!'

Sourtoe cocktail

CANADA

The story goes that back in the 1920s, Louie Linken, a miner and rum runner in Canada's Yukon Territory, had one of his severely frostbitten toes amputated with a woodcutting axe by his brother Otto in order to prevent gangrene. For reasons best known to himself, Louie elected to preserve the toe in his cabin in a jar of alcohol. Fifty years later, in 1973, a local eccentric named Captain Dick Stevenson stumbled across the blackened toe while cleaning the cabin and, after discussing the gruesome find with friends, decided to instigate the Sourtoe Cocktail Challenge at a bar in Dawson City. Since then more than 65,000 people have taken on the challenge. The rules are simple: customers pay $5 plus the price of the drink to guzzle the liquor of their choice from a beer glass containing the severed human toe, which at some point must touch the drinker's lips. As the Sourtoe Cocktail Club states: 'You can drink it fast, you can drink it slow, but the lips have gotta touch the toe'.

Alas, according to the club, Linken's toe only survived for another seven years until, in 1980, miner Garry Younger, while attempting an unprecedented thirteenth glass of Sourtoe champagne, toppled backwards on his chair and inadvertently swallowed the appendage, which was never recovered. A replacement toe was donated by a loyal customer who had undergone an amputation due to an inoperable corn while number three, from another victim of frostbite (an occupational hazard in the Yukon), was also swallowed accidentally. The anonymously donated toe number four was stolen by an unscrupulous souvenir hunter, five and six were donated by an old local in return for free drinks for his nurses, toe seven was an amputation due to diabetes, and number eight arrived in a jar of alcohol with the message: 'Don't wear open-toe sandals while mowing the lawn'. The ninth toe was the victim of an unsavoury incident in 2013 when an American visitor ordered the famous cocktail, deliberately gulped the entire drink – toe and all – and slammed down $500, the fine for swallowing the toe. Happily the bar had a replacement toe to hand in the freezer, but the episode led to the fine being raised to $2,500.

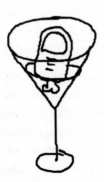

As many as thirty people a day attempt the Sourtoe Cocktail Challenge at the Downtown Hotel, where the pickled toe still resides. The latest toe is described as resembling a leathery piece of jerky with a jagged yellow toenail attached, but with people regularly bequeathing their toes to the bar in their wills, the dubious tradition looks set to continue for many years to come.

INGREDIENTS
- 1oz of alcohol
- 1 dehydrated human toe
- 1 large shot of courage

METHOD
Pour the drink into a beer glass and add a human toe. Down the drink, making sure your lips touch the toe but preferably without swallowing it.

Recipe: *www.atlasobscura.com*

Elephant dung beer

JAPAN

In 2013, Japanese brewery Sankt Gallen launched a beer using coffee beans that had passed through an elephant's digestive system. They called it *Un, Kono Kuro*, a play on '*unko*', the Japanese term for 'crap'.
The beans, called Black Ivory, were carefully hand-picked from the dung of elephants at Thailand's Golden Triangle Elephant Foundation. Just 35 grams of the beans cost over $100 – meaning that the beer would work out at around $1,100 per keg – mainly because 33 kilos of beans in the mouth yields just one kilo of usable beans at the other end. Despite its jumbo price tag, the first batch of elephant dung stout sold out within a matter of minutes.

A contributor who tasted the beer for website RocketNews24. com wrote enthusiastically: 'After taking my first sip there was an initial bitterness that got washed over by a wave of sweetness. Following that, a mellow body rolled in and spread out through my mouth. Usually people talk about aftertaste when drinking beer but with *Un, Kono Kuro* the word afterglow is much more appropriate. After downing the last drop, slowly rising from my throat and mouth was that afterglow. The combination of bitter and sweet stayed fresh and lingered in my head. It was a familiar aroma that accompanied me through the entire beer.'

Mass production would seem unlikely, however, as it could take a long, long time waiting for elephants to eat, digest and poop out the necessary amount of coffee beans. Besides, how much would you have to pay someone to sift through mountains of elephant shit in search of tiny beans? It must be like looking for a needle in a very smelly haystack.

Beard beer

Of more than 1,600 strains of yeast, only a few can ferment sugars into alcohol. In the never-ending quest to introduce exotic new beers to the market, Newport, Oregon, brewery Rogue Ales had tested dozens of different yeasts without success, only to find that the answer was staring at them in the face – in the beard of their award-winning brewmaster John Maier.

One day, someone joked that Maier's luxuriant facial hair, which had not been shaved for over thirty years, might be the ideal medium for growing yeast. Since yeast is a fungus more readily found in rotting fruit, mouldy hay, feathers or bird droppings, he could have taken offence at the suggestion but instead he willingly plucked nine hairs from his beard and sent them to a California laboratory for testing and culturing. When the results came back, they showed that his beard hairs were indeed growing yeast – a unique blend of wild yeast and Rogue's popular house variety, Pacman. As the yeast fungi thrive in breweries and his beard had attended over 15,000 brews in the course of his twenty-year career, he had almost certainly collected the Pacman yeast as part of his job while the wild yeast had probably taken up residence in his beard after he had eaten some fruit or maybe a passing robin.

So the brewery turned the yeast from Maier's beard into a Belgian-style ale. Some hailed it as an act of creative genius but others thought it sounded the most disgusting thing ever. To allay drinkers' concerns, Rogue's president Brett Joyce explained: 'You're not really drinking a beard, you're drinking a great beer that happens to have a yeast that comes from a beard.'

When Rogue Beard Beer hit the shelves in 2013, the reaction was cautiously enthusiastic with comments ranging from 'pretty damned delicious' and 'amazingly refreshing' to 'repugnant' and 'a smell of dirty dishwater'. For those who liked it, the good news is that Maier announced he had no intention of ever shaving off his beard, meaning that there will be no shortage of raw material.

Snake wine

SOUTH-EAST ASIA

For most of us, putting something in our drink is limited to a couple of ice cubes or a slice of lime or lemon but in China, Vietnam and other parts of south-east Asia they drink wine that has been infused with a whole snake – preferably a highly venomous one. The good news about snake wine is that the venom dissolves in the alcohol and is therefore rendered harmless – that is, provided the snake is dead in the first place. For if the bottle or jar is not airtight, a live snake can effectively hibernate in the wine by lowering its metabolism and heart rate and therefore still possess the ability to give the drinker a nasty shock. In 2013, a woman from China's Heilongjiang Province was bitten on the hand by a pit viper which leaped out of the bottle when she went to add more alcohol to a brew that had already been fermenting for three months. And in 2001, a Chinese villager was killed by a snake wine attack.

Snakes are believed to possess many medicinal qualities and the wine, which was first recorded in Chinese medicine around 771BC, is advertised as being able to boost health and virility and cure everything from back pain to hair loss. So when asked to name their poison, Chinese people often go for snake wine even though westerners who have tried it for the first time reported no Viagra-like benefits and described the taste as 'bland, like licking stamps'. Others have said it smells 'like one might imagine a sumo wrestler's loincloth might after a tough fight'.

At first glance, you could mistake snake wine for a nice rosé until you realize that the pink hue is the result of the reptile's blood.

A safer version – a sort of snake wine lite – is three-lizard liquor, where a handful of geckos and other small lizards are crammed into the bottle of alcohol. The Chinese believe that geckos possess powerful energy and so in theory the more geckos that can be squeezed into the bottle, the more energizing the drink. It sounds as if it makes Red Bull look like Horlicks. In addition, many traditional Asian medicine men are convinced that three-lizard liquor counters the forces of evil. What more could you require from a drink?

INGREDIENTS

- 1 dead snake
- 1 bottle of rice wine
- Mixed herbs
- Small birds, lizards and insects (optional)

METHOD

Place a large dead venomous snake into a glass jar or bottle of rice wine. Do not simply assume that the snake will drown in the liquid. For extra flavour, you can add smaller snakes, insects, birds, lizards and medicinal herbs. Leave to steep for several months. Drink the wine from small shot glasses.

Recipe: *wikipedia*

Three penis wine
CHINA

___

The next time you need a stiff drink or a Valentine's Day gift that your loved one will always remember, look no further than a refreshing bottle of *Tezhi Sanbian Jiu*, otherwise known as three penis wine. Sold inexpensively in supermarkets around Shanghai, it is a rice wine that has been fermented with three types of animal penis – seal penis, deer penis and Cantonese dog penis. All are popular ingredients in Chinese medicine as they are supposed to boost male potency and virility. There is no record of what effect it has on women. As you would expect from its name, it is the ultimate liquor.

Most of us would be reluctant to allow an alcoholic drink that contains the essence of a single penis to pass our lips, let alone one with three, but what's the worst that could happen? Since the major ingredient is deer (four parts deer to one of seal and one of dog), at the very least we should be able to put on a good show in the rutting season, culminating with a starring role in *Autumnwatch*.

Chicago mixologist Michael Rubel described the taste of three penis wine as 'like a vintage port that had gone really, really bad and hung out with some sherry and some prunes. I think the dog penis really comes through on the finish, which is quite prolonged.' He went on to create a cocktail – the Three Penis Swizzle – combining three penis wine, lime juice, syrup, Aperol, Vida mezcal, and grapefruit bitters. Before you ask, he used plastic stirrers.

Surprisingly, three penis wine does not come in a box.

Baby mice wine

CHINA

If you like a wine with body, this should be just the ticket. For it has fifteen bodies – of baby mice, so young their eyes are still closed and their fur has not yet grown, which have been poured alive into rice wine and left to drown and ferment for at least a year.

Baby mice wine is used as a traditional health tonic in China and Korea, where it can supposedly cure a range of ailments including asthma and liver disease. It is so potent that two small glasses are apparently enough to get you hammered, although it is difficult to imagine anyone going back for a second glass because, as if the prospect of drinking a wine that has been infused with the corpses of baby mice were not sufficiently off-putting, it is said to taste like raw gasoline. Obviously you would need to have tasted gasoline to be able to make the comparison, which probably tells you all you need to know about the type of people who drink baby mice wine.

INGREDIENTS
- 15 baby mice
- 1 bottle of rice wine

METHOD

Take the baby mice, which should be no more than three days old, and tip into a bottle of rice wine. Leave to stand in a dark, dry place for between 12 and 14 months, by which time the corpses will have sunk to the bottom and they are allegedly safe for public consumption. Pour into a glass. Swallowing the mice is optional.

Recipe: *www.cracked.com*

Faeces wine

KOREA

Fed up with waiting for that bruise to heal or nursing a broken foot? Try an invigorating glass of *Ttongsul*, a medicinal rice wine whose special ingredient is the fermented faeces of a human child.

The wine, which is 9 per cent alcohol, uses the faeces of children around the age of six because, according to Korean medicine men, their poo does not smell. These people have clearly never had to escort a six-year-old to the toilet following an excess of pizza and ice cream at a birthday party. The faeces come from children who have been given anthelmintic beforehand to get rid of roundworm, thus making their poo nice and 'pure'. This is comforting to know. One medicine man laments that because of human rights issues he can no longer obtain children's faeces by himself. Instead he says he obtains them from young, open-minded mothers.

Ttongsul has been used in Korea for centuries to make cuts and bruises disappear, mend broken bones and even cure epilepsy. Its devotees claim that while someone suffering a nasty fall might be hospitalized for twenty days, a regular dose of the magic wine could heal the patient in half the time. The production of *Ttongsul* was believed to have died out in the 1960s but a few traditionalists have kept it going underground. They use a mix of non-glutinous

and glutinous rice to make the wine because non-glutinous
has the required amount of protein needed for the fermenting
process and glutinous rice improves the taste. And when you're
making faeces wine, anything that improves the taste is not to be
dismissed lightly.

The end result is a milky green colour with a slightly sour taste.
One of the few journalists ever to have sampled *Ttongsul* (luckily
for modern-day Koreans, most of them have never heard of it) said:
'It tastes like rice wine but when I breathe out of my nose it smells
like poo'.

The medical claims of *Ttongsul* are, of course, unproven, but one
thing is certain. Drinking faeces wine may not cure your broken
foot but it will definitely make you forget about it for a few
seconds.

INGREDIENTS

- 1 child's poo
- 1 large jug of water
- 3 cups of non-glutinous rice
- 1 cup of glutinous rice
- 1/4 of a Chinese yeast ball

METHOD

After first removing the poo from the child's bottom (it is best if this is allowed to take place naturally), keep it refrigerated for three to four days. Then put it in a bucket, add the water, stir vigorously until most of the poo has dissolved, and leave the solution to stand for 24 hours. Mix the non-glutinous and glutinous rice, boil the rice and drain it through a sieve. Crumble the yeast and pour into a pot with the rice. Add the concentrated poo water to begin the process of fermentation. Keep it for a week at a temperature of 30–37°C, perhaps by wrapping the pot in a blanket. Strain the liquid before drinking.

Recipe: *Daily Mail*

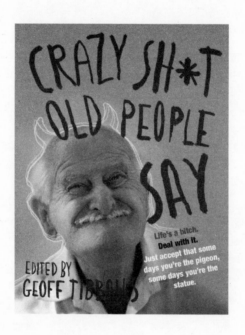

Crazy Sh*t Old People Say

GEOFF TIBBALLS

Available to buy in ebook and paperback

With old age comes grey hair, dodgy knees, a sudden passion for re-runs of *Murder, She Wrote*, and an apparent God-given licence to speak one's mind and be generally offensive without fear of retribution.

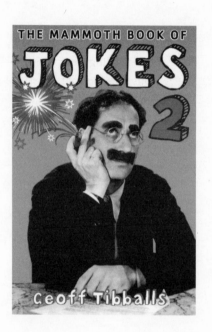

The Mammoth Book of Jokes 2

GEOFF TIBBALLS

Available to buy in ebook and paperback

From the man behind the bestselling *Mammoth Book of Jokes*, comes an all-new, enormous collection of fantastic jokes – indexed and categorised to help find the right joke for the right occasion, from Bar-Mitzvahs to bar-rooms.

Bigger, better, and even bulkier than before, *The Mammoth Book of Jokes 2* is the consummate collection, with jokes on every subject under the sun, from lawyers to low-energy light bulbs.

The Mammoth Book of One-Liners

GEOFF TIBBALLS

Available to buy in ebook and paperback

A collection of 10,000 side-splitting one-line jokes arranged in categories from bestselling humour editor Geoff Tibballs.

'Is my wife dissatisfied with my body? A small part of me says yes.'

'Letting the cat out of the bag is a whole lot easier than putting it back in.'

'I read somewhere that 26 is too old to still live with your parents. It was on a note, in my room.'

The Mammoth Book of Weird News

GEOFF TIBBALLS

Available to buy in ebook and paperback

A humorous collection of hundreds of funny news stories, whacky phenomena, and hilarious blunders and gaffes from around the world, such as: the woman who smuggled 75 live snakes in her bra; the man who held a funeral for his amputated foot; the radioactive cat which got mistaken for a bomb; the human tongue that got served up in a hospital; the X-ray that revealed E.T.'s face in a duck; the youth who woke to find a bullet in his tongue; the tortoise that set a house on fire; and many more.